JC   Douglas
585
.D6   Anatomy of liberty

THE CREDO SERIES

VOLUMES ALREADY PUBLISHED

THE CREDO SERIES

PLANNED AND EDITED BY
RUTH NANDA ANSHEN

THE ANATOMY
OF LIBERTY

The Rights of
Man Without Force

BY

WILLIAM O. DOUGLAS

A TRIDENT PRESS BOOK
NEW YORK 1963

Prepared under the supervision of
POCKET BOOKS, INC.

CONTENTS

THE CREDO SERIES

Its Meaning and Function

The Credo Series suggests that an epoch has come to an end, an epoch in which our best knowledge has been dimmed with boredom or darkened by destruction. We have felt for too long that this must be the very nature of life; this is the way life is, and to such a degree that life has consented to shrink from its own terrors, leading us to a deep apostasy of the heart and a crucifixion of our natural aspiration for experience and growth.

The absolute has surrendered to the relative. Our era of relativity, however, whether in science or in morals, does not allow us to assume that relativity implies an absence of ground to stand on, and therefore a relaxation of all effort toward foundations. "There is no firm ground," the dominant malaise of our time, this acceptance of non-finality, summons us to a heightened task. For the failure of formulated absolutes leaves the absolute requirement to evaluate again that uncaptured reality which contains and guides the total meaning of our existence.

The Credo Series hopes to unlock a consciousness that at first sight may seem to be remote but is proved on acquaintance to be surprisingly immediate since it shows the need to reconcile the life of action with the life of contemplation, practice with principle, thought with feeling, knowledge with being, and work, no longer a form of punishment as in the Judaeo-Christian tradition, but accepted as a way toward the growth and realization of the self in all its plenitude. For the whole meaning of self lies within the observer and its shadow is cast naturally on the object observed. The fragmentation of man from his work, the being of man into an eternal and temporal half, results in an estrangement of man from his creative source, from his fellows and from himself.

The symbol of *The Credo Series* is the Eye of Osiris. It is the inner Eye. Man sees in two ways: with his physical eyes, in an empirical sensing or *seeing* by direct observation, and also by an indirect envisaging. He possesses in addition to his two sensing eyes a single, image-making, spiritual and intellectual Eye. And it is the *in-sight* of this inner Eye that purifies and makes sacred our understanding of the nature of things; for that which was shut fast has been opened by the command of the inner Eye. And we become aware that to believe is to see.

Thus, it is suggested, there may be born a sharpened vision, which comes from seeing reality as the incarnation of associations and affinities with something beyond the visible self. For it is our hope to show the human relevance of ideas, the ways in which knowledge can help us to live in the immediate and real world by pointing to the confluence of man and his vocation, of subject and object, by reverencing the curious and mysterious metabolism between man and matter, the sacred nexus between the person and his work, and by asking whether the freedom now released through the creative energies of mankind will bring salvation or destruction, the answer to which will depend upon the aims we cherish.

The Credo Series submits that the universe itself is a vast entity where man will be lost if it does not converge in the person; for material forces or energies, or impersonal ideals, or scientifically objectified learning are meaningless without their relevance for human life and their power to disclose, even in the dark tendencies of man's nature, a law transcending man's arbitrariness.

For the personal is a far higher category than the abstract universal. Personality itself is an emotional, not an intellectual, experience, and the greatest achievement of knowledge is to combine the personal within a larger unity, just as in the higher stages of development the parts that make up the whole acquire greater and greater independence and individuality within the context of the whole. Reality itself is the harmony which gives to the component particulars of a thing the equilibrium of the whole. And while physical observations are ordered with direct reference to the experimental conditions, we have in sensate experience to do with separate observations whose correlation can only be indicated by their belonging to the wholeness of mind.

It is our endeavor to show that man has reached a turning point in consciousness, that his relationship with his creative self demands a clarification that can widen and deepen his understanding of the nature of reality. Work is made for man, not man for work. This Series hopes to demonstrate the sacramental character of work which is more easily achieved when the principal objects of our attention have taken on a symbolic form that is generally recognized and accepted: in other words, when there is an established iconography relating to the meaningful interpretation of man and his vocation. This suggests a "law" in the relationship of a person and his chosen discipline: that it is valuable only when the spiritual, the creative, life is strong enough to insist on some expression through

symbols. For no work can be based on material, techno-
logical or physical aspirations alone.

The human race is now entering upon a new phase of
evolutionary progress, a phase in which, impelled by the
forces of evolution itself, it must converge upon itself and
convert itself into one single human organism dominated
by a reconciliation of knowing and being in their inner
unity and destined to make a qualitative leap into a higher
form of consciousness that would transcend and comple-
ment individual consciousness as we know it, or otherwise
destroy itself. For the entire universe is one vast field,
potential for incarnation, and achieving incandescence
here and there of reason and spirit. What to some is mys-
tery and inscrutability, to others symbolizes and declares
the very nature of the cosmic process. And in the whole
world of *quality* with which category by the nature of our
minds we necessarily make contact, we here and there
apprehend pre-eminent value. This can be achieved only
if we recognize that we are unable to focus our attention
on the particulars of a whole without diminishing our
comprehension of the whole, and of course conversely, we
can focus on the whole only by diminishing our comprehension of the particulars which constitute the whole.

This Series is designed to present a kind of intellectual
autobiography of each author, to portray the nature and
meaning of the creative process for the creator and to show
the relevance of his work to the feelings and aspirations
of the man of flesh and bone. This Series endeavors to
reflect also the influence of the work on the man and on
society and to point to the freedom, or lack of freedom, to
choose and pursue one profession rather than another.
It attempts to emphasize that the creator in any realm
must surrender himself to a passionate pursuit of the hid-

den meaning of his labors, guided by deep personal intimations of an as yet undiscovered reality.

These volumes endeavor to indicate that it is impossible to know what constitutes a good society unless we know what defines a good individual. The self is determined by the values according to which it subordinates and integrates the rest of its values. If the values be transient, so is the self. If the values be dispersed and incoherent, so is the self. If they are organic and integrated, so is the self. The unity of human personality is its soundness. The unified self cannot be understood in terms of its constituent parts as dissected away from each other. So that finally what we see and what we do are no more and no less than what we are.

It is the effort of *The Credo Series* to define the new reality in which the estrangement of man and his work, resulting in the self-estrangement in man's existence, is overcome. This new reality is born through the reconciliation of what a man *knows* with what a man *is*. Being itself in all its presuppositions and implications can only be understood through the totality, through wholeness. St. Paul, who, like Isaiah before him, went into the market place not to secularize truth but to proclaim it, taught man that the "new creation" could be explained only by conquering the daemonic cleavages, the destructive split, in soul and cosmos. And that fragmentation always destroys a unity, produces a tearing away from the source and thereby creates disunity and isolation. The fruit can never be separated from the tree. The Tree of Life can never be disjoined from the Tree of Knowledge for both have *one and the same* root. And if man allows himself to fall into isolation, if he seeks to maintain a self segregated from the totality of which he is a necessary part, if he chooses to remain asunder, unrelated to the original context of all created things in which he too has his place—including his own labors—then this act of apostasy bears fruit in the demiurgical presumption of *magic*, a form of animism in which man seeks an authority of the self, placing himself above the law of the universe by attempting to separate the inseparable. He thus creates an unreal world of false contexts after having destroyed or deserted the real. And in this way the method of analysis, of scientific objectivity, which is good and necessary in its right place, is endowed with a destructive power when it is allowed to usurp a place for which it is not fitted.

The naturalist principle that man is the measure of all things has been shattered more than ever in our own age by the question, "What is the measure of man?" Post-modern man is more profoundly perplexed about the nature of man than his ancestors were. He is on the verge of spiritual and moral insanity. He does not know who he is. And having lost the sense of who and what he is, he fails to grasp the meaning of his fellow man, of his vocation, and of the nature and purpose of knowledge itself. For what is not understood cannot be known. And it is this cognitive faculty which is frequently abrogated by the "scientific" theory of knowledge, a theory that refuses to recognize the existence of comprehensive entities as distinct from their particulars. The central act of knowing is indeed that form of comprehension which is never absent from any process of knowing and is finally its ultimate sanction.

Science itself acknowledges as real a host of entities that cannot be described completely in materialistic or mecha-nistic terms, and it is this transcendence out of the domain of science into a region from which science itself can be appraised that *The Credo Series* hopes to expose. For the essence of the ebb and flow of experience, of sensations, the richness of the immediacy of directly apprehended knowledge, the metaphysical substance of what assails our being, is the very act itself of sensation and affection and therefore must escape the net of rational analysis, yet is intimately related to every cognitive act. It is this increasing intellectual climate that is calling into birth once more the compelling Socratic questions, "What is the purpose of life, the meaning of work?" "What is man?" Plato himself could give us only an indirect answer: "Man is declared to be that creature who is constantly in search of himself, a creature who at every moment of his existence must examine and scrutinize the conditions of his existence. He is a being in search of meaning."

Theory and life always go together. An organic conception of man and his work, man and society, man and the universe, is portrayed in First Corinthians 12 when Paul relates the famous story of the strife that once broke out between the parts of the human body. They refused to fulfill their special functions within the organism until they finally learned that they are all parts of one body and can exist and function only as such. For they all breathe together. And by so doing subordinate themselves to the presentation of the whole body. What may be an explanation of organic life in the human body may be transferred to the life in the universe and to the relationship between the interior and the exterior, for all is permeated by the life-giving creative power—by unity.

The authors in this endeavor are aware that man in the twentieth century finds himself in the greatest revolution since the discovery of agriculture. They show, each in his own way, that part of the meaning of our present turmoil may indeed lie in its being the means to reconcile thought and action, to overcome the parochialism of dogmas that only isolate man from man and man from the implicit meaning of his chosen profession. Our effort is to create an image of man intelligible and unitary, a microcosmic mirror of the greater macrocosm of which he is a part and in which he has his legitimate place in relation to the whole. For even the extraordinary successes of scientific predictions, the fruits of man's ingenuity in inventing the scientific method, seem comprehensible only on the basis that the human mind possesses an inherent logic closely parallel with the structure of the external world itself.

The very interdependence of the observer and the participant can no longer be ignored as part of the essential value of things. To take a definitive example from modern cosmology, it is challenging indeed to note that there is a most unusual connection between the existence of stars and the laws that govern the atomic nuclei. Emphasis is placed upon the existence, not the properties, of stars. For everyone expects the properties of stars and atomic nuclei to be related. It is the *connection* with the *existence* of stars that is so reassuring—and indeed surprising.

From this it is evident that there is present in the universe a *law* applicable to all nature including man and his work. Life itself then is seen to be a creative process elaborating and maintaining *order* out of the randomness of matter, endlessly generating new and unexpected structures and properties by building up associations that qualitatively transcend their constituent parts. This is not to diminish the importance of "scientific objectivity." It is, however, to say that the mind possesses a quality that cannot be isolated or known exclusively in the sense of objective knowledge. For it consists in that elusive humanity in us, our self, that knows. It is that inarticulate awareness that includes and *comprehends* all we know. It consists in the irreducible active voice of man and is recognized only in other things, only when the circle of consciousness closes around its universe of events.

The experience of the modern mind has been expressed in terms of conflict produced by false dualisms, disruption, self-destruction, meaninglessness, purposelessness and desperation. This character of our time has found its expression in literature, in art, in existential philosophy, in some forms of natural science, in political demonologies, and is explored in the psychology of the unconscious. Our authors hope to indicate that through a quickening of awareness man can overcome this dualism and can rise to face the meaning of life and work, keeping his mind and energies awake at full stretch. Such knowledge—that form of knowledge which cannot be disjoined from being—will enable man to embrace life with passion and to work with devotion. It will enable him to absorb experience with his whole nature and thereby to fill a want that is satisfied neither by action alone nor by thought alone. This unity of *being* and *doing* has a justifiable claim to be called a form of enchantment since through it men, who might otherwise give in to the malice of circumstances and conditions, find their old powers revived or new powers stirring within them, and through these life is sustained, renewed and fulfilled.

Man is now confronting himself with the compelling need to create an organic identification between what he *is* and what he *does*. For only in this way can the threat of conformism and the treachery of abstraction, the plight of the modern mind, be conquered. This split, inherited from the seventeenth century, between the transitive and the intransitive, between the creator and the process of creativity, has blunted man's appetite for experience. Language itself in our time has failed because man has forgotten that it is the mother of thought, because of its analytical emphasis, and thus lacks ready means to convey associations, emotional or imaginative, that cluster around a subject and give to it a distinctive personal significance. In other words, the symbols by which man lives and has his being, that "tacit coefficient" * of articulate knowledge that is unanalyzable, now knocks at the portals of consciousness waiting to be admitted. For human nature loses its most precious quality when it is robbed of its sense of things beyond, unexplored and yet insistent.

The Credo Series belongs to those ideas that are intuitively conceived and that originate in spheres of a spiritual order and surprise thought, as it were, compelling it to transform its inherited notions conformably with its enlarged vision of the nature of things. It is as though the authors of the Series were recovering this reality out of a memory of a lost harmony, a memory latent in the soul and not distilled from the changing things of mere physical observation. In this way the inner unity of the known and the knower may be preserved, and the almost mythic intuition of reality thereby related to its conceptual and rational forms of expression. For man, unlike a machine, is an organism existing as an end in itself. He *is* the system on which causal explanations are based and to which they have to return; he *is* a historically existent whole, a four-dimensional entity, and not merely an abstraction from which statements about phenomena are deducible under the guise of eternity.

* See the classical work, *Personal Knowledge,* by Michael Polanyi for an enlarged meaning of the nature of reality. (Chicago University Press, 1958)

Our hope is to point to a new dimension of morality—not that of constraint and prohibition but a morality that lies as a fountainhead within the human soul, a morality of aspiration to spiritual experience. It suggests that necessity is laid upon us to infer entities that are not observed and are not observable. For an unseen universe is necessary to explain the seen. The flux is seen, but to account for its structure and its nature we infer particles of various kinds to serve as the vertices of the changing patterns, placing less emphasis on the isolated units and more on the structure and nature of relations. The process of knowing involves an immaterial becoming, an immaterial identification, and finally, knowledge itself is seen to be a dependent variable of immateriality. And somewhere along this spiritual pilgrimage man's pure observation is relinquished and gives way to the deeper experience of awe, for there can be no explanation of a phenomenon by searching for its origin but only by discerning its immanent law—this quality of transcendence that abides even in matter itself.

The present situation in the world and the vast accretion of knowledge have produced a serious anxiety, which may be overcome by re-evaluating the character, kinship, logic and operation of man in relation to his work. For work implies goals and intimately affects the person performing the work. Therefore the correlation and relatedness of ideas, facts and values that are in perpetual interplay could emerge from these volumes as they point to the inner synthesis and organic unity of man and his labors. For though no labor alone can enrich the person, no enrichment can be achieved without absorbing and intense labor. We then experience a unity of faith, labor and grace which prepares the mind for receiving a truth from sources over which it has no control. This is especially true since the great challenge of our age arises out of man's inventions in relation to his life.

Thus *The Credo Series* seeks to encourage the perfection not only of man's works but also and above all the fulfillment of himself as a person. And so we now are summoned to consider not only man in the process of development as a human subject but also his influence on the object of his investigation and creation. Observation alone is interference. The naïve view that we can observe any system and predict its behavior without altering it by the very act of observation was an unjustified extrapolation from Newton's *Celestial Mechanics*. We can observe the moon or even a satellite and predict its behavior without appreciably interfering with it, but we cannot do this with an amoeba, far less with a man and still less with a society of men. It is the heart of the question of the nature of work itself. If we regard our labors as a process of shaping or forming, then the fruits of our labors play the part of a mold by which we ourselves are shaped. And this means, in the preservation of the identity of the knower and the known, that cognition and generation, that is, creation, though in different spheres, are nevertheless alike.

It is hoped that the influence of such a Series may help to overcome the serious bifurcation of function and meaning and may show that the extraordinary crisis through which the world is passing can be fruitfully met by recognizing that knowledge has not been completely dehumanized and has not totally degenerated into a mere notebook over-crowded with formulas that few are able to understand or apply.

For mankind is now engaged in composing a new theme. Life refuses to be embalmed alive. Life cannot abjure life;

nothing that lives is born out of nothingness. But nothing, either, can preserve its form against the ceaseless flux of being. Life never manifests itself in negative terms. And our hope lies in drawing from every category of work a conviction that non-material values can be discovered in positive, affirmative, visible things. The estrangement between the temporal and non-temporal man is coming to an end, community is inviting communion and a vision of the human condition more worthy of man is engendered, connecting ever more closely the creative mind with the currents of spiritual energy which breaks for us the bonds of habit and keeps us in touch with the permanence of being in all its plenitude through our work.

And as, long ago, the Bearers of Bread were succeeded by the Bearers of Torches, so now, in the immediacies of life, it is the image of man and his vocation that can rekindle the high passion of humanity in its quest for light. Refusing to divorce work from life or love from knowledge, it is action, it is passion that enhances our being.

We live in an expanding universe and also in the moral infinite of that other universe, the universe of man. And along the whole stretched arc of this universe we may see that extreme limit of complicity where reality seems to shape itself within the work man has chosen for his realization. Work then becomes not only a way of knowledge, it becomes even more a way of life—of life in its totality. For the last end of every maker is himself.

"And the places that have been desolate for ages shall be built in thee: thou shalt raise up the foundations of generation and generation; and thou shalt be called the repairer of the fences, turning the paths into rest." *

—RUTH NANDA ANSHEN

* Isaiah, 58:12

THE ANATOMY OF LIBERTY:
The Rights of Man Without Force

MY CREDO

The central problem of our time—one that is shared by all races and nationalities—is to discover the things, the qualities, and interests that peoples have in common so that durable institutions can be designed for mankind's survival. The ideological differences in the world have produced on each side of each curtain a press that searches for areas of conflict between men and between nations rather than for opportunities for harmony. A press can create a national mood; and each one has done so, with the result that every community the world over is now filled with suspicion. The result is ominous, for the nuclear holocaust is the ultimate end-product of modern conflicts. It is easy to find disagreeable qualities in one's neighbor—let alone in the Russians and the Chinese.

A measure of the suspicion extant in the world can be found in every field. A law professor in Moscow would dare say few things complimentary about the Anglo-American legal system; and there are not many here who would venture to praise anything "communistic." Yet the two opposing systems at the legal, engineering, cultural, medical, or community level have much in common.

Laws vary greatly, but the concept *of justice remains bright in every land. Throughout history people have*

xxiii

honored the just king. In China the ruler, whatever his ideology, always had a "mandate" from Heaven. Throughout history people have also honored the just judge. The appetite for justice is indeed a cementing influence among all races, whatever language they speak, whatever the color of their skin.

In Jerusalem I heard the Israeli Supreme Court say, "It is better that ten guilty persons be acquitted than that one innocent person be convicted."

In Calcutta I learned that no statement of a person under arrest made to a policeman is admissible in evidence.

In Ulan Bator I discovered that Mongolia allows no ex post facto *law.*

In Baghdad I found a passion for equal justice under law under the revolutionary regime of the late Abdul Karim Kassem who was cruelly caricatured as neo-communist.

In Lahore I saw the same golden threads in Islamic jurisprudence that we have in our own.

In Alma-Ata I learned that counsel is assigned in every criminal case to an accused who does not have one.

In Belgrade I discovered that under Yugoslav law even prisoners have two weeks' vacation.

On all the continents of the world I learned that the people fear the nuclear holocaust and desire to live in peace; that in spite of cultural, ideological, and racial differences, we, the people of the world, have more in common than we have in conflict.

Those who want to build a Free Society where none has ever existed need instruction in the anatomy of liberty and guidance along the way. The West must send teachers of law, government, and history by the tens of thousands to provide this leadership. Moreover, as James J. Wadsworth, *former United States Ambassador to the United Nations, recently said, "If we have confidence that our way of doing things is better than that of our competitors, we don't have to prove it by force. What we desperately need to do is to develop a force of example which proclaims our inward force of character."* [1]

We who believe in liberty must indeed live our ethic if it is to be an important influence abroad.

Liberty at home means nothing in this nuclear age if liberty is no more than a mirage to those in other lands. The United States has poor wards and precincts, even poor States; and those economic imbalances are problems with which our federalism deals. Federalism at the regional and world level must perform a like function lest poverty-ridden areas produce revolutions of despair. A world order requires much more. The task of this age is to search for building blocks out of which a consensus *among nations can be found—a* consensus *that will provide the ways and means of survival.*

We can respect one another even though we fall far short of total agreement. Respect is the start of cooperation; and cooperation often ends in friendship. The antagonistic attitudes towards the Germans and Japanese rather quickly changed and friendship now flourishes where hate recently possessed us.

A world without war is worth the supreme effort. It can be achieved in this century if, instead of expending our energies on exploiting deterrent power, we make an understanding of the anatomy of liberty both at the local and at the world level our preoccupation. That is my credo.

—WILLIAM O. DOUGLAS

[1] "Let's Be Adult," *Sat. Rev.*, Dec. 29, 1962, p. 9.

I am indebted to Dagmar Hamilton and Jared G. Carter for their invaluable assistance on the manuscript and to the law students and faculty at the University of Baghdad who listened patiently to the lectures out of which this book grew and whose questions and comments enriched it.

I
THE INDIVIDUAL AND THE STATE

> *"In a free government the security for civil rights must be the same as that for religious rights. It consists in the one case in the multiplicity of interests, and in the other in the multiplicity of sects."*
>
> —FEDERALIST No. 51

MAN'S STRUGGLE for liberty has no date for its beginning or for its end. In the past it has been primarily a contest against a ruler: sometimes from a colonial regime, at other times, a person of the same race and color as the subjects. The oppressor has appeared as a king, a dictator, a religious group, a politburo, an army. Today one measure of liberty is the extent to which the individual can insist that his government live under a Rule of Law. Another is the immunity of the individual when he shakes his fist at the authorities and defies them if they fail to follow the supreme law.[1] Still another measure of liberty is the degree to which society affords the individual an opportunity to develop as an integrated human being, healthy in body and soul, with a mind unfettered, with ideas, conscience, and belief inviolate from governmental interference, with a chance for individual preferment and opportunity.

1

The Declaration of Independence written by Thomas Jefferson and adopted on July 4, 1776, is a Declaration of the Rights of Man: "We hold these truths to be self-evident, that all men are created equal, that they are endowed by their Creator with certain unalienable Rights, that among these are Life, Liberty and the pursuit of Happiness."

Men do not acquire rights from the government; one man does not give another certain rights. Man gets his rights from the Creator. They come to him because of the divine spark in every human being.

Jefferson went on to say, "That to secure these rights, Governments are instituted among Men, deriving their just powers from the consent of the governed"—not from on high, not from a king, but from "the consent of the governed." That is basic to any Free Society.

The Declaration of Independence also says that every people has the right to revolution. It is the right of the people to abolish an old government, to form a new government, and to organize it in such form as seems to them best for their safety and happiness.

That is the essence of the American Declaration of Independence. It has contributed greatly to the cause of the equality of man the world over.

Our Constitution, unlike the British one, is written. The Bill of Rights—which makes up the first Ten Amendments—contains the chief protection for human rights. But the body of the Constitution has certain guarantees which the Founding Fathers thought were rights that should be secured to all people.

The guarantees expressed in the Bill of Rights are no monopoly of the West. India, in its constitution, recognizes many of them. Their roots are deep in Eastern philosophy as well as in Western experience. One can trace them to the teachings of the Koran, to the moral precepts of the Bible, to the words of Buddha, to the philosophy of the Hindus.

The philosophy of the Bill of Rights was put into enduring words by an Arab scholar and philosopher, Dr. Charles Malik of Lebanon. Dr. Malik, who was a member of the Commission on Human Rights of the United Nations, helped draft a Declaration of Human Rights for the United Nations. Dr. Malik stated what he deemed to be the fundamental principles of civil rights:

> 1. The human person is more important than the racial, national, or other group to which he may belong;
> 2. The human person's most sacred and inviolable possessions are his mind and his conscience, enabling him to perceive the truth, to choose freely, and to exist;
> 3. Any social pressure on the part of the State, religion or race, involving the automatic consent of the human person is reprehensible;
> 4. The social group to which the individual belongs may, like the human person himself, be wrong or right: the person alone is the judge.[2]

Dr. Malik was not, of course, addressing himself to American constitutional law. But what he said summarizes the philosophy of our Bill of Rights and of all constitutions which put the individual above the State and above the group. The State cannot require the citizen to sacrifice his belief and his conscience in order to conform to what the State thinks is best. Nor can the group to which he belongs punish him for expressing disagreement or dissent from the policy of the group.

These four points of Dr. Malik state, indeed, the vital

differences between the Western philosophy toward government and the communist philosophy.

A man cannot be punished through application of an *ex post facto* law. What is done lawfully today cannot be made a crime tomorrow with a retroactive effect. In some countries there is no regard for that principle. In the Hungarian uprising of 1956, many youngsters 16 and 17 years old were convicted. But under the Hungarian law they could not be executed because they were under 18 when they committed the crime. So they were held until they reached 18 years of age and then executed.

On July 1, 1961, the Soviets passed a new law applicable to crimes involving foreign exchange. This new law carried the death penalty. After July 1, 1961, the Presidium of the Supreme Soviet issued a special edict which made that law specifically applicable to two defendants whose crimes had been committed prior to July 1, 1961. The trials were held and the July 1, 1961 law was used to send the two defendants to death.

The communist world is not the only transgressor. The Chang government that was in control of South Korea in 1960 used *ex post facto* laws in an organized way. It created a Special Court [3] (later known as the Revolutionary Court) [4] to enforce an *ex post facto* law. This law, promulgated December 31, 1960, punished "unjust acts" committed in connection with the election held on March 15, 1960; and the penalties for violation ran from seven years' imprisonment to death.[5] The military junta that took control May 16, 1961, passed the Illicit Fortune Disposition Law [6] which also was retroactive and punished, *inter alia,* those who had accumulated fortunes of designated amounts "by availing himself of the position and powers of a public office or political party, or by fraud or other illegal means." It was enacted June 15, 1961, and reached back to the period beginning July 1, 1953, and ending May 15, 1961.

Those included in the term "illicit fortune accumulations" must register within a ten-day period after the effective date of the new law. They must account for the "illicit fortune" pursuant to certain formulas included in the law. They must pay taxes in arrears plus penalties up to 400 per cent of the arrears. The illicit fortune accumulators who are notified of their duty to pay under the law and who "deliberately" default "shall be subject to death, life imprisonment, imprisonment for not less than three years, or to fines amounting to not more than twice the amount notified." Those who "conceal" or "transfer" property to evade the law "shall be subject to death, imprisonment for life or not less than ten years, and all their property shall be confiscated." The law was administered by a seven-man committee that made the investigations and returned the indictments.

Our Constitution outlaws the bill of attainder, which is a measure passed by the legislature—not by a court— that adjudges a man guilty, imposes a sentence of death or imprisonment on him, or subjects him to other penalties. In Ghana, leaders opposed to the government have been banished from the country by a bill of attainder. Another modern bill of attainder appeared in South Korea. The Chang government promulgated on December 31, 1960,[7] a law which deprived designated classes of persons of civil rights for committing anti-democratic acts. Those acts were defined as those that are "inconsistent with principles of democracy and which infringe upon or limit the basic rights of the people guaranteed by the Constitution or any other laws." The civil rights withdrawn were (a) the

qualifications for becoming a public official and (b) the
right to vote and to be elected. These penalties were imposed by *ad hoc* administrative agencies and reached far
down into administrative offices as well as into higher public offices. In America, if a man is to be punished, it must
be after a judicial trial in which he can be heard and in
which he is represented by counsel. He is to be tried by
a court, not by a legislative body. Once Congress charged
certain government employees with being subversive. It
added a provision to an appropriation bill that no part of
the appropriation should be used to pay these individuals
and that they should not thereafter be on the government
payroll. The case reached the Supreme Court in a suit
brought by these men for their salary.[8] The law was held
unconstitutional because it was a bill of attainder—an act
of a legislature adjudging guilt.

There are other provisions in the main body of our Constitution that protect the rights of men. No religious oath
shall be required for the holding of a public office. In America a Moslem, Hindu, or a person of any other faith can
be President. In 1960 we elected a Catholic President. It
is a powerful force in the life of a people to realize that
a man's religion has no bearing on his qualifications for
public office. Even an agnostic or atheist cannot be barred
from public office.[9]

Each of the fifty States of the United States has its own
Constitution. At the time of the adoption of the federal
Constitution, each had numerous guarantees of individual
rights. So the Bill of Rights was passed *only* to limit the
power of the central government. But as time passed there
were changes in the American constitutional system. In
the 1860s we had a civil war. One of the results of the
Civil War was the adoption of the Fourteenth Amendment

which, among other things, provides that no State shall deprive "any person of life, liberty, or property without due process of law, nor deny to any person within its jurisdiction the equal protection of the laws." The first of these two provisions is known as the Due Process Clause of the Fourteenth Amendment; and the second is known as the Equal Protection Clause. The Due Process Clause has been judicially construed to incorporate within it some of the specific provisions of the Bill of Rights. Among the rights so incorporated are those expressed in the First Amendment. Those First Amendment rights concern freedom of speech, freedom of the press, freedom of assembly, and freedom of religion.

Freedom of expression, even by those whose ideas the government may despise, comes high in the American scheme of values. No one in American history has better expounded the political theory behind this guaranty than Thomas Jefferson. He wrote in 1779:

> That the opinions of men are not the object of civil government, not under its jurisdiction; that to suffer the civil magistrate to intrude his powers into the field of opinion and to restrain the profession or propagation of principles on supposition of their ill tendency is a dangerous fallacy, which at once destroys all religious liberty, because he being of course judge of that tendency will make his opinions the rule of judgment, and approve or condemn the sentiments of others only as they shall square with or suffer from his own; that it is time enough for the rightful purposes of civil government for its officers to interfere when principles break out into overt acts against peace and good order; and finally, that truth is great and will prevail if left to herself; that she is the proper and sufficient antagonist to error, and has nothing

to fear from the conflict unless by human interposition disarmed of her natural weapons, free argument and debate; errors ceasing to be dangerous when it is permitted freely to contradict them.[10]

Jefferson's theory and the idea espoused by the Britisher, John Stuart Mill, have common ground. Mill wrote, "If all mankind minus one, were of one opinion, and only one person were of the contrary opinion, mankind would be no more justified in silencing that one person, than he, if he had the power, would be justified in silencing mankind." [11]

This does not mean of course that a person can slander or libel another. Exceptions for slander and libel as well as obscenity have deep roots in American law. Yet to that generality there are exceptions. Under an Act of Congress every radio station must "afford equal opportunities" to all candidates who run for public office. The radio station, however, has "no power of censorship" over the broadcast. The result is that the radio station is not liable for defamatory statements that a candidate makes.[12]

Nor may libel and slander be used as a weapon against those who criticize the operations of government. "One of the prerogatives of American citizenship is the right to criticize public men and measures—and that means not only informed and responsible criticism but the freedom to speak foolishly and without moderation." [13] One court, in order to protect this First Amendment right, has held that "fair and honest criticism of the acts of a public official in a matter of public interest are not libelous unless they are written maliciously." [14] That states the preferred view, for otherwise the law of libel would swallow much of the

First Amendment and make perilous the actions of the opposition in criticizing those in power.

A man who bears arms against his government or who takes any preparatory measure towards that end can be punished; but revolution as a subject of discourse may not be outlawed any more than a defense, criticism, or advocacy of any political, philosophical, or religious creed. Bigamy may be outlawed; but the discussion of it, its defense and its approval, may not be made illegal.

Ideas are, of course, dangerous—the most dangerous forces in the world. Advocacy of an idea may be an incitement too powerful for any resistance. Every speech is a form of incitement—sometimes an incitement to action, sometimes to meditation. The strength of democracy lies in the freedom to express—and to debate—ideas.

The United States has not always been faithful to these principles of freedom of expression. In one case, those who banded together to teach Marxism were convicted of a criminal conspiracy [15] in spite of the fact that nothing but teaching was involved—no overt acts of sabotage, espionage, or subversion. In another case, being an "active" member of the Communist Party was sustained as a crime; and "advocacy" of its political creed was said to be punishable.[16] Those decisions cannot be squared with the Jeffersonian philosophy.

Their philosophy is reflected in the anti-communist law promulgated by the military government of South Korea, July 3, 1961, which imposed imprisonment for those "praising, encouraging or cooperating with anti-State organizations, or their constituent members." [17]

Jefferson believed that dangerous as advocacy and the excitement of ideas were, there was even greater danger in suppression. A government that enters upon a program of suppression has its special views of the public good in mind. But what may seem good to the government may not always be the best for the people. Moreover, the airing of views and their advocacy is healthier than their suppression. Martyrs are made when people are not allowed to speak. The clash of argument is the best way known to man for separating false from enduring ideas.

Freedom to learn is another aim of freedom of expression. It is, indeed, one of the values in a free society. In Nebraska, a local law made it a crime to teach any child who had not passed the eighth grade any subject in any language other than English. One teacher who taught the German language was prosecuted and convicted. The Court reversed the judgment, saying that the law conflicted with the right of teachers to teach, of students to learn, and of parents to control the education of their children.[18]

Dr. Robert Oppenheimer recently spoke of the growing importance of free, unfettered minds: "By knowing more of nature and a little, pitifully little, of ourselves, we know how to make things and do things which otherwise we should not have known how to make or do; and by these increased abilities and powers we in general offer to men a far wider range of choices as to what and how they are to do, what and how they are to make. This has, of course, altered the face of the earth." [19]

In communist lands scientific inquiry is not limited, though inquiry into the humanities is. A mature civilization allows unfettered minds not only to promote some state objective such as armaments or science or industrialization, but also to develop whole and integrated personalities who by the flowering of ideas realize their full potentials.

The theory is that people raised in an atmosphere where ideas—whether in politics, economics, or art—are not limited, become courageous and self-reliant. Then they are enabled to fulfill the responsibilities of self-government. Where ideas or schools of thought are suppressed, people become less self-reliant; indeed, they are apt to become timid. Unused to ideas, they are untrained for emergencies that new problems often create.

Freedom of speech in America means that no man need get a license from the government in order to make a speech.[20] But in South Korea the military junta that took control in 1961 greatly restricted political rights of prior officeholders by requiring that they obtain from an administrative agency of the new government a "judgment of qualification" in order to run as candidates for office, to make election speeches, to hold political meetings, or to support or obstruct political activities of political parties. The penalties for doing any of those acts without a "judgment of qualification" are fine and imprisonment. As of March, 1962, over 4,000 Koreans had been sent into political exile under this law for the Purification of Political Activities.[21] In effect this law requires a license for one to engage in political activities—a measure designed to improve the public morality, but one that is at war with the ideals of the Free Society.

Freedom of assembly is close kin to freedom of speech. Freedom of speech might be an empty right if people could not gather to hear the speaker. Freedom of assembly and freedom of speech indeed go hand-in-hand. The abuse of speech—as, for example, inciting a riot—can be punished

but the right itself cannot be. The right peaceably to assemble for public discussion and debate for political action
and community activities is firmly entrenched. This right
extends even to those as unpopular as the communists.[22]
Freedom to petition the government is also unlimited.

Historically the right to assemble was secondary to the
right to petition, the latter being the primary right. But
today the right of peaceful assembly is considered equally
as fundamental as other First Amendment rights. Freedom
of assembly extends not only to political organizations, but
also to the almost innumerable groups engaged in social,
economic, religious, educational, or artistic endeavor. And
the First Amendment goes beyond protecting such organizations while they are actually "assembled." It protects
each member's associational interest in belonging to his
group, whether it be popular or unpopular. Legislation or
legislative investigation requiring organizations to disclose
their membership is properly applied only to an organization shown to be engaged in conduct subject to governmental regulation; *i.e.,* to an organization which itself is
engaged in unlawful conduct. Were the rule otherwise,
government could ransack even the files of churches looking for criminals or ideological strays. Government then
would have its nose in matters which the First Amendment
places beyond the pale. Its invasion of the sacred precincts
of privacy would give it a totalitarian character at war with
the democratic ideal.

Freedom of the press is likewise protected by the First
Amendment. Freedom of the press, like freedom of speech,
has many values to the editor or speaker, to the reader or
listener, to society as a whole. The book, the speech, the
pamphlet, open new horizons for people. They are essen-

tial for the scientist, the philosopher, or the administrator, as well as for an informed electorate.

The classic statement came from John Milton in the famed *Areopagitica,* a book which Oliver Cromwell and his Parliament condemned in 1644. Milton wrote:

> . . . books are not absolutely dead things, but do contain a potency of life in them to be as active as that soul was whose progeny they are; nay, they do preserve as in a vial the purest efficacy and extraction of that living intellect that bred them. I know they are as lively, and as vigorously productive, as those fabulous dragon's teeth; and being sown up and down, may chance to spring up armed men. And yet, on the other hand, unless wariness be used, as good almost kill a man as kill a good book. Who kills a man kills a reasonable creature, God's image; but he who destroys a good book, kills reason itself, kills the image of God, as it were in the eye. Many a man lives a burden to the earth; but a good book is the precious life-blood of a master spirit, embalmed and treasured up on purpose to a life beyond life. 'Tis true, no age can restore a life, whereof perhaps there is no great loss; and revolutions of ages do not oft recover the loss of a rejected truth, for the want of which whole nations fare the worse.
>
> We should be wary therefore what persecution we raise against the living labours of public men, how we spill that seasoned life of man, preserved and stored up in books; since we see a kind of homicide may be thus committed, sometimes a martyrdom, and if it extend to the whole impression, a kind of massacre; whereof the execution ends not in the slaying of an elemental life, but strikes at that ethereal and fifth essence, the breath of reason itself, slays an immortality rather than a life.[23]

Throughout history, the battle to let books live—especially if they are controversial—has been ceaseless. There are always people and governments who would censor that which is critical of the prevailing social, religious, or political philosophy. In South Africa, under the guise of an "anti-sabotage" law, newspapers and other informational media have been prohibited from publishing any statements, past or previous, of persons whose names appear on a special governmental roster known as the "gag list." This list, which includes persons from all races and walks of life, also silences the Zulu Nobel peace prize winner, Albert Luthuli. Because fear of ideas tends to breed even greater fear of ideas, the "gag list" is ever-expanding. The list of proscribed books in Ireland, though drawn up by different standards, is even more ominous. For it includes most of Thomas Wolfe, *Anthony Adverse* by Hervey Allen, *Elmer Gantry* by Sinclair Lewis, *No Star Is Lost* by James T. Farrell, *Silver Nutmeg* by Norah Lofts, *The White Tower* by Ramsey Ullman, to mention only a few.

By nature, the printed word can multiply the power of an idea by disseminating it to the many. Licensing of the press, like restrictions on speech, has not been uncommon. Traffic in ideas has ever been a concern to dictators. Political or religious dissenters are, indeed, the plague of every totalitarian regime.

Censorship has had a long history in the Western world. The list is long; the examples are almost legion. Licensing of the press continued in England until 1694. Book burning is as old as books. There are still censors in most lands. Sometimes religious groups publish proscribed lists to advise their members which books should not be read.

Censorship is alien to the American system. In a clas-

sic case Minnesota condemned as a nuisance, and allowed
to be enjoined, any "malicious, scandalous and defamatory" newspaper or magazine. A paper called *The Saturday Press* was condemned under this statute as a nuisance,
and its owners and publishers were perpetually enjoined
from publishing it. The Court set the injunction aside as
being an unconstitutional restraint on freedom of the
press. More recently the Court struck down a procedure
under which the "Rhode Island Commission to Encourage
Morality in Youth" effectively censored books objection-
able to a majority of the Commission by merely notifying
the distributor of the majority's decision and threatening
prosecution if he did not remove the banned book from
his shelves.[24] These laws laid a previous restraint on publication, a device used in colonial days to suppress criticism
and stifle opposition to those in power. The press in
America may be sued—civilly and criminally—for wrongs
inflicted or crimes committed. But it may not be censored.

There has been much dispute in the United States concerning the power of municipalities or states to censor
movies. In 1915, the Court held that the movies were not
within the guarantee of freedom of the press.[25] But the
Court changed its position in 1952, and held that movies
were under the protection of the First Amendment.[26] Yet
in 1961, the Court held in a five-to-four decision that
censorship of movies was not *per se* unconstitutional.[27]
That is a decision which cannot be squared with the First
Amendment.

Movies, like television, sometimes deal with political
ideas, with social problems, with theological matters, with
economic or educational questions. The censor who, with
the stroke of the pen, outlaws a movie or who, with scis-
sors, deletes parts of a film decides what ideas are good

and which ones are bad for society. The movie censor, like the censor of novels or poetry, also acts as arbiter of the arts and decides what is in good taste, what is vulgar, what is cheap. Freedom of expression through acting, through music, through the medium of the theatre, should be accorded the same constitutional dignity as freedom of expression through books, newspapers, or political tracts. The American theory is that the people need no office of oversight in any of these fields. Their applause or their rejection is the ultimate test, not a censor's notion of morality, ideology, or artistic worth.

Censorship of the press is only one historic method of suppression. Taxation of the press was another. Of course, a publisher can be required to pay the same kind of taxes that all citizens pay as a part of the price of civilization. But the taxes that have an invidious incidence are those which historically were known in America as "taxes on knowledge." They were rampant in England during the eighteenth century, and generated powerful opposition. The stamp tax laid on the cheaper papers that reached the masses had the effect of stifling their circulation or greatly curtailing it.

That kind of a tax is unconstitutional in the United States. One case involved a tax of two per cent on the gross receipts derived from advertisements carried in a newspaper when, and only when, the newspaper had a circulation of more than 20,000 copies per week. The law was aimed at a powerful group that was opposed to the regime that was in control of Louisiana in 1934. The Court said:

> The tax here involved is bad not because it takes money from the pockets of the appellees. If that were all, a

wholly different question would be presented. It is bad because, in the light of its history and of its present setting, it is seen to be a deliberate and calculated device in the guise of a tax to limit the circulation of information to which the public is entitled in virtue of the constitutional guaranties. A free press stands as one of the great interpreters between the government and the people. To allow it to be fettered is to fetter ourselves.[28]

Newspapers and magazines which are free to print the whole truth, even when it may be critical of those in power, serve the cause of an enlightened public opinion. By presenting the pros and cons of issues, they help keep public opinion in a state of thoughtful ferment.

Though the United States has not suffered from legal restraints on freedom of the press, the press has served in recent years less and less of its historic role to inform and educate people and to debate current issues. Several influences have caused that decline. One is government secrecy. Information is classified as "confidential" at such a rate it is estimated that the weekly supply from the Pentagon alone would form a pile higher than the Empire State Building in New York City. Another factor is the growing complexity of government, increasingly technical aspects of the problems with which it deals, and a greater reliance on experts for guidance in the solutions to the problems raised by the age of nuclear fission and outer space. Still another is the widening range of world affairs, the emergence of new nations, the mounting tensions, the clash of power blocs—much of which is concealed by the veil of ignorance created by our inability to speak and read many critical foreign languages. Also important has been the tendency among the press to become more and more a money-making project, not an educational force.

Books may serve as powerful agencies of social, economic, or political reform. They may enable people to gain a keener insight into society and its problems. The same is true of the newer media—radio, television, and motion pictures.

Freedom of expression, like other liberties, does not arrive neatly packaged. Those long held under colonial rule were often made criminals when they shouted their protests to their rulers. When they acquired independence, the new leaders often reacted to criticism in the manner of their old rulers. Menderes, who took criticism of his government as a personal affront, laid a heavy hand on the Turkish press. Nkrumah in Ghana used his new powers to drive his political opposition out of the country or to send them to jail. The give-and-take of a continuing dialogue is the very essence of the Free Society. Yet it is sometimes the last of all the freedoms to be realized.

Freedom of expression was given temporary tolerance in China when Peking early in 1957 said, "Let one hundred flowers bloom and one hundred schools of thought contend." But the flowering and discussion that resulted caused alarm, and a Stalin-like regime was reimposed on the people. The press was chastised not for criticizing the regime, but for reporting statements of people who did criticize it; faculties were purged of politically unreliable professors; writers were charged with a plot "against Party leadership of culture"; and as a sequel there were many public "confessions" to "subversive acts of rightists." [29]

Freedom of expression is mostly a stranger to Russia. *Dr. Zhivago,* by Boris Pasternak, though only mildly critical, received at home an ominous silence. Yet the yeast of freedom works wherever man is articulate. Yevtushenko

—not yet thirty—published *Stantzia Zima* on Stalin's death:

> So it turns out the doctors weren't guilty?
> Then why have the people been treated like that?
> It's a scandal before the whole of Europe.[30]

Babi Yar is a ravine near Kiev where the Nazis massacred 100,000 Jews. The incident was blurred by the Soviet government and reference to it in terms of anti-Semitism was banned. In 1961 Yevtushenko put the account of Babi Yar in immortal words:

> There is a rustling of wild grass over Babi Yar.
> The trees look fearsome, like judges.
> Everything here screams in silence. . . .

> *   *   *

> Let the "Internationale" thunder forth
> When the last anti-Semite on earth
> Has been buried for good.[31]

The Soviet press roared denunciation. But Yevtushenko said, "I will remain firm to the end and never become an unctuous boot licker." [32]

Eventually, Yevtushenko was forced to delete two lines of *Babi Yar,* and two new lines were added, in order to make the U.S.S.R. appear less anti-Semitic. At the same time, he was subjected to severe attack because of the publication of his uncensored autobiography in France. Other writers denounced him, and his speaking engagements in the United States were suddenly cancelled. It is significant, however, that five of his poems, including *Babi*

Yar, were set to music by Shostakovich in his *Thirteenth Symphony,* and that the readings and performances of his poems must have touched the hearts of many Russians who admired his courage and daring in attempting to express freely his own views of life and government in the Soviet Union.

When Yevtushenko in 1963 published his memoirs in France, the Soviet press demanded that he and other young nonconformist writers be barred from further trips abroad until they "mature politically." What he wrote in his memoirs was critical of the Bolshevik Revolution. He said, *inter alia:*

> Russian people would rather work than analyze. With heroic stubbornness rarely found in history they built power station after power station, factory after factory. They worked with bitterness so that the roar of machines, tractors and bulldozers muffled the cries and sighs that tore through the barbed wire of the Siberian concentration camps.

It is out of episodes of this character that freedom of expression is won.

The Western history of freedom of expression, which is now mostly forgotten, was written slowly and painfully by men and women who have their counterparts in the minorities of China and Russia. These minorities will, in time, not be denied.

Gandhi, speaking in quite a different context, expressed the philosophy of the American guarantee of freedom of expression:

> I do not want my house to be walled in on all sides and

my windows to be stuffed. I want the cultures of all lands
to be blown about my house as freely as possible. But I
refuse to be blown off my feet by any. Mine is not a religion of the prison house. It has room for the least of
God's creations, but it is proof against insolent pride of
race, religion, or color.[33]

Religious differences, like racial ones, have produced
heated clashes between peoples. The old wars between
Christianity and Islam are but one example. A minority,
seeing itself about to be governed by a majority of another
religious faith, may be filled with fear. The fear of a secular
state, governed by a Hindu-dominated parliament, led to
the partition of India and the creation of Pakistan. If,
however, that formula were applied faithfully, India
would be further partitioned. There are Christians, Sikhs,
Buddhists, and Parsees in India. Each sometimes fears a
religious majority made up of non-believers in their own
faith. Such were the fears when America won her independence, for there were many religious groups here. The
American solution shows a workable alternative to partition along religious lines; and it has worked well whatever
may be the religious faith of the President, of the Judges,
or of the state or federal legislature.

There are two aspects of freedom of religion with which
our First Amendment deals. First is the provision that government shall not establish a religion. Second is the provision that government shall not prohibit the free exercise
of religion.

In America, we once had an established church. That
was in the colonial period under the British who made the
Anglican Church the official preferred church. It was supported by taxation. Only its clergy could officiate at mar-

riages and baptisms. Other religious sects were in existence and held their services. But they existed only as a
matter of favor, as is true in some nations today.

In 1779, shortly after the Revolution, the Anglican
Church was disestablished. But the constitutions which the
new States adopted usually provided that public taxes
should go to the support of churches. And those early constitutions also discriminated against Catholics, Jews, and
atheists.

Soon an effort was made to put all Christian churches
on an equal footing by supporting all of them by taxation.
Virginia made this proposal in 1784. The measure had
distinguished supporters. But Thomas Jefferson and James
Madison were against it. They marshaled the opposition;
and Madison made their voices articulate in his *Memorial
and Remonstrance Against Religious Assessments*. The
proposal was defeated and Madison's *Remonstrance* has
gone down in American history as the most eloquent brief
ever written on the need for separating Church and State
and keeping them separate. Madison wrote:

> Rulers who wished to subvert the public liberty, may
> have found an established clergy convenient auxiliaries.
> A just government, instituted to secure & perpetuate it,
> needs them not. Such a government will be best sup-
> ported by protecting every citizen in the enjoyment of
> his Religion with the same equal hand which protects
> his person and his property; by neither invading the equal
> rights of any Sect, nor suffering any Sect to invade those
> of another. . . .
> Whilst we assert for ourselves a freedom to embrace,
> to profess and to observe the Religion which we believe
> to be of divine origin, we cannot deny an equal freedom
> to those whose minds have not yet yielded to the evi-

dence which has convinced us. If this freedom be abused, it is an offence against God, not against man: To God, therefore, not to men, must an account of it be rendered. . . .

The Religion then of every man must be left to the conviction and conscience of every man; and it is the right of every man to exercise it as these may dictate. This right is in its nature an unalienable right. It is unalienable; because the opinions of men, depending only on the evidence contemplated by their own minds, cannot follow the dictates of other men: It is unalienable also; because what is here a right towards men, is a duty towards the Creator. It is the duty of every man to render to the Creator such homage, and such only, as he believes to be acceptable to him. This duty is precedent both in order of time and degree of obligation, to the claims of Civil Society. Before any man can be considered as a member of Civil Society, he must be considered as a subject of the Governor of the Universe. . . .

The preservation of a free government requires not merely, that the metes and bounds which separate each department of power may be invariably maintained; but more especially, that neither of them be suffered to overleap the great Barrier which defends the rights of the people. The Rulers who are guilty of such an encroachment, exceed the commission from which they derive their authority, and are Tyrants. The People who submit to it are governed by laws made neither by themselves, nor by an authority derived from them, and are slaves.[34]

The present status of the law is that neither a state nor the federal government can pass laws which aid one religion, aid all religions, or prefer one religion over another; nor levy any tax in any amount, large or small, which is used to support any religious activities or any religious institution; nor prescribe a prayer for the opening of public schools.[35] America is a religious nation and its people believe in prayer. But the First Amendment bars the communities from having a government official do their praying for them. For the prescription by government of a prayer is one step toward establishing a religion; and when government takes that step it exerts a divisive influence, as no one prayer can satisfy all sects.

Public funds can support public projects. But schools run by religious groups may not receive public funds, whether the funds go to pay salaries, build buildings, buy books, or finance a secular activity of the school. Some say that if public funds paid the salaries of teachers of mathematics in religious schools, there would be no violation of the Constitution. That is not true. A religious school is indivisible. What aids one part of its activities saves money for promotion of its other activities.

The First Amendment has a broad reach and includes the exotic forms of religion, as well as the more conventional types.[36] That aspect of religious freedom arose in a controversy over a requirement of public schools that children salute the flag. Jehovah's Witnesses—a religious sect—object to the flag salute and refuse to perform it. They believe that it is forbidden by the commands of the Scriptures contained in Exodus 20:3-5:

> Thou shalt have no other gods before me.
> Thou shalt not make unto thee any graven image, nor any likeness of any thing that is in heaven above, or that is in the earth beneath, or that is in the water under the earth.
> Thou shalt not bow down thyself unto them, nor serve them.

A West Virginia school board expelled children of Jehovah's Witnesses for refusing to salute the national flag as part of the daily school exercise. Suit was brought by the parents to enjoin the school authorities from continuing to exact the flag-salute ceremony as a condition of their children's attendance. If the requirement violated the First Amendment, the parents would prevail, for, as we have seen, the Due Process Clause of the Fourteenth Amendment makes the guarantee of religious freedom good against the states. The Court held that saluting the flag required a member of this religious sect to "bear false witness to his religion." [37]

There has been much litigation over the authority of municipal or state authorities to license, tax, and in other respects control the activities of religious groups. The litigation has involved mostly those who go from door to door distributing religious literature or soliciting purchases of it. Sometimes they stand on street corners and seek to interest passers-by in their tracts. People who practice their religion in this way may not be discriminated against. For example, if other religious groups are entitled to hold open meetings in the parks, such people must be included.[38]

Municipalities have sought to exact a license tax from these itinerants for their soliciting activities. The Court held that tax unconstitutional under the First and Fourteenth Amendments. "The hand distribution of religious tracts is an age-old form of missionary evangelism—as old as the history of printing presses." "The power to tax the exercise of a privilege," said the Court, "is the power to control or suppress its enjoyment." [39]

By like reasoning, a city ordinance forbidding any person to knock on doors, ring doorbells, or otherwise summon to the door the occupants of any residence for the purpose of distributing handbills or circulars was held unconstitutional as applied to a person distributing advertisements for a religious meeting.[40]

Licensing requirements for these religious sects have also been struck down [41] since the power to grant, or to withhold, a license to practice a religion is a power of life or death over that religion. In New York City, a municipal ordinance required a permit from the police commissioner for a person to preach or expound a religious faith in a public place. A Baptist minister spoke outdoors without a permit and was convicted for that omission. The Court reversed his conviction, holding that a licensing system so vague and general as to give the police commissioner power to pick and choose among religions, laid a forbidden burden on the exercise of religious liberty.[42]

Licensing provisions as applied to religious workers are a previous restraint upon the free exercise of religion. When the licensing authority has unbridled discretion to determine whether a particular group is a religious group, there is censorship in the worst form. The fact that there would be a judicial remedy for abuse of the authority of the licensing agency is not enough. If one has to obtain a permit to perform his religious practices, his exercise of religion is not free. Freedom to practice a religion is as much a part of religious freedom as freedom to believe. The state may regulate the times and manner of solicitation so as to prevent frauds upon the people. The state may regulate the use of its streets and parks. But any such regulation that touches religious practices must be "narrowly drawn to define and punish specific conduct as constituting a clear and present danger to a substantial interest of the state." [43]

Neither speech, press, nor religion can be used to cause

riots, to make disturbances, to tie up traffic in city streets. These are matters that can be regulated by the authorities. Religion cannot be used to justify immoral acts and practices. Immoral practices traveling under the cloak of religion may be outlawed by government. In criminal prosecutions for bigamy, the defendants pleaded that they were merely practicing polygamy which was one of their religious precepts. The Court held that polygamy was offensive to the American community and could be outlawed.[44]

That is a dangerous test. It was applied in recent cases upholding the constitutionality of laws prohibiting certain types of commercial transactions on Sundays.[45] Those laws, as applied to minorities who worship on a different day than the majority, mean that members of those faiths must respect the religious scruples of the majority, and not do on Sunday acts which are offensive to the community. That means in effect that the dominant religious group may bring "the minority to heel because the minority, in the doing of acts which intrinsically are wholesome and not antisocial, does not defer to the majority's religious beliefs." [46] It would seem that a legislature of Christians should no more make religious minorities conform to their weekly regime than a legislature of Moslems or a legislature of Hindus should make Christians bow to theirs.

The Soviets used the same formula in a more extreme way. A religious group known as Pentecostals were charged with teachings and activities "hostile to humanity." Witnesses testified that disease was spread by religious practices which, in the manner of the Bible, included: "communion services in which bread was passed from hand to hand and wine drunk from one vessel, and the washing of feet without the water being changed." [47] Baptizing people in cold water—in the manner of John the Baptist—was also said to be dangerous to health. So under the guise of health a sturdy religious group was crushed in Russia. Later, members of the same sect were given five-year prison terms for suggesting to other members that they refrain from joining the army and from listening to the radio, and that they read nothing except the Bible.

In a multi-racial, multi-religious country, cultural autonomy is necessary for a harmonious Free Society. Gandhi and Nehru, speaking for the Hindus, and Iqbal, speaking for the Moslems, recognized this as they faced the problems of an India freed of colonial control.[48] Partition was the alternative finally chosen. America developed a harmonious whole out of many cultural diversities by putting religion beyond the reach of legislatures and by keeping legislatures out from under the clerical thumb. If it had been partitioned among Anglicans, Catholics, and Quakers, its prospects would have been infinitely fewer.

The people of all continents have had problems with the police. Searches and arrests by police are governed in America by the Fourth Amendment and various procedural rules. With rare exceptions an officer cannot make an arrest without going to a judge and getting a warrant. If he sees a crime being committed, he can of course make an arrest. But if he merely thinks that there has been a crime committed, he must gather his evidence and submit it to a judge who makes an independent determination. The same procedure is necessary if a home or an office is to be searched. If a police officer proceeds on his own to make an arrest or a search, he is a trespasser and no evidence so obtained may be used in the subsequent trial. This requirement of the Fourth Amendment is applicable to the States by reason of the Due Process Clause of the Fourteenth Amendment.[49] The privacy of the home, guaranteed by the constitution of Venezuela, has been undermined by a subterfuge. Since that guarantee restrained only the police, health officers were used to break down doors and make arrests, a practice that has received some sanction in the United States.

A critical problem has involved the tapping of telephone wires. While the Court is composed of only nine Justices, and while more than nine Justices have thought that wire tapping was a search that required a warrant under the Fourth Amendment, those nine have not sat on the Court at the same time. The result is that the Court has refused to require the police to get a search warrant, based on probable cause, in order to tap a person's telephone.[50] Wire taps are, however, regulated by federal law. Congress passed a statute which makes wire-tap evidence inadmissible in federal trials.

The police in all lands like to detain people and hold them incommunicado in order to get confessions. Our Federal Rules of Criminal Procedure provide that an officer who makes an arrest shall take the arrested person "without unnecessary delay" before the nearest available magistrate. Production of a suspect before a judicial officer serves several functions:

It gives the arrested person the right to get bail, which is protected by our Eighth Amendment.

It brings him to the public eye and makes possible a contact with his family, his friends, and his lawyer. It puts an end to the possibility of detention incommunicado.

Prompt production before a magistrate is, therefore, essential to protection of the rights of the accused. Everyone is presumed innocent until proven guilty. But the police have often assumed the opposite and subverted a lawful arrest to oppressive ends.

Preventive detention is allowed in many nations even in time of peace—Argentina, Brazil, Burma, Colombia, Ghana, India, Malaya, South Africa, not to mention, of course, communist countries. Some societies are deemed to be so fragile that those in power are authorized to lock up without trial people who endanger internal stability or security. Thus in Burma a person acquitted of a charge in a criminal case may be arrested and detained on the same charge, when his detention is deemed necessary for the preservation of public order and security. One theory expressed by the Burma courts is that people who are frightened at testifying in open court will nonetheless give the police reliable information concerning the subversive character of the accused. That, however, is too glib an answer. For the "faceless informer"—one who dares not come into the open and undergo cross-examination—has been a curse to liberty throughout history. His abuses, as we shall see, are the reason why the right of confrontation was written into the Sixth Amendment of the United States Constitution.

The reading of the decisions from the courts of those nations where preventive detention is allowed shows, in the main, two things. First, power is a heady thing, as governments tend to enlarge their power as much as possible with the result that they overstep the limits of their authority and take short cuts to avoid irksome or burdensome restrictions which the law governing protective detention places on them. Second, courts sitting in review of acts of preventive detention usually have been, with notable exceptions, zealous in keeping the authorities within line and watchful that the procedural safeguards of protective detention be strictly adhered to. This has been particularly true of the Indian courts; they have administered the law impartially and have insisted that all of its procedural guarantees be strictly observed.

Preventive detention in the United States has sometimes been undertaken by Governors of States in time of peace through declarations of martial law. But, as we shall see, those orders are reviewable by the judiciary. Though a riotous condition may warrant the arrest of people, it does not justify their detention, except pending a trial in a civilian court. Even in time of war a civilian can be tried by a military tribunal only in extreme situations. Preventive detention of some American citizens of Japanese ancestry was undertaken in the United States during World War II, an action, which we shall see, was held to be unauthorized.

In the early days of the Civil War, Lincoln, as Commander in Chief, issued an order: "That during the existing insurrection and as a necessary measure for suppressing the same, all rebels and insurgents, their aiders and abettors, within the United States, and all persons discouraging volunteer enlistments, resisting militia drafts, or guilty of any disloyal practice, affording aid and comfort to rebels against the authority of the United States, shall be subject to martial law, and liable to trial and punishment by court-martial or military commissions."

Milligan, a civilian resident in Indiana, was arrested by the military, tried by a military commission, and sentenced to be hanged. The charges against him were conspiring against the United States, affording aid and comfort to the enemy, inciting insurrection, and discouraging enlistments —all crimes defined by Congress and made punishable by the civil courts. Milligan, by a petition for a writ of *habeas corpus,* challenged the authority of the military commission to try him. The case reached the Court in 1866 and, in one of the most momentous decisions in its long history, it held that the trial of Milligan by a military commission was unconstitutional. (*Ex parte Milligan,* 4 Wall. 2.)

Though Indiana was, at the time of Milligan's arrest, in a theatre of military operations, the civil courts were open and functioning. It was held that so long as they were open, martial law could not be used to suspend the civil rights of citizens—an important one being the right to trial by jury. "Martial law," the Court said, "cannot arise from a threatened invasion. The necessity must be actual and present; the invasion real, such as effectually closes the courts and deposes the civil administration." (*Idem,* p. 127.) The Court went on to say that if there was a foreign invasion or civil war and the civil courts were actually closed and it was impossible to administer criminal justice according to law, the military could govern. "As necessity creates the rule, so it limits its duration; for if this government is continued after the courts are reinstated, it is a gross usurpation of power. Martial rule can never exist where the courts are open, and in the proper and unobstructed exercise of their jurisdiction." (*Idem,* p. 127.)

Those who conspired to take Lincoln's life were tried by a military commission and executed by its order. James Speed, the Attorney General in Lincoln's second Administration, maintained the legality of that action, even though the civil courts were open and functioning. But Edward Bates, Lincoln's first Attorney General, bitterly assailed the action, calling it illegal and unconstitutional. That has been the view of the scholars. It would seem clear that under the rule of *Ex parte Milligan,* such a trial could not be constitutionally justified.

The *Milligan* case has never been overruled. It stands as unimpeached authority for the view that, even in time of war, the right of the citizen to normal judicial procedure and to the guarantees of the Fifth and Sixth Amendments is secure, if he is outside the actual zone of warfare and if the administration of justice through the civil courts remains in fact unobstructed.

The police the world over have at times used torture and more subtle instruments of persuasion to get prisoners to confess. Every man can be "broken." There is a point where the nervous system can take no more pain, shock, or fatigue; where it will pay any price for relief. A few minutes, a few days, or a few weeks may be required, depending upon the individual and the torture device that is employed. Once that point has been reached, the accused becomes, for the moment, putty in the hands of the police and will admit what they charge and sign what they want.

Historically, these police practices were used primarily against the poor, the weak, the uninfluential. Sometimes the victims were racial minorities; sometimes, political or religious minorities. The need of the police to bring men promptly to a magistrate is reflected in a recent decision where a man was held thirty hours and then confessed. A conviction based on that confession was set aside.[51]

The practice of holding men incommunicado was so common in India that a statute was enacted excluding from criminal trials all statements to the police. If the accused wants to make a confession, he makes it before a magistrate; and it is only that confession that is admissible at the trial. This is the most enlightened procedure of any country.

The technique of obtaining evidence through torture has vicious ancillary consequences. As stated in Report of the Indian Police Commission and Resolution of the Government of India, ". . . the police officer is unduly impelled by the statistical test to try to make his investigation end in conviction." Hence the temptation to bolster the case with false evidence. Hence the temptation to get pleas of guilty. The pattern is apparently the same the world over. In a larceny trial in China in the 1920s the accused was stretched on a wheel until he confessed. The prosecution then scurried around to find corroborating evidence.

The Soviet policy shows the other extreme. Down to December, 1958, a man could be held incommunicado for 63 days, at the end of which he had to be brought to trial. Since 1958, it has been possible for the prosecutor to get extensions of time that may add up to six months. This dominance of the police in Soviet Russia is at war with the institutions of a Free Society.

The Fourth Amendment is only one check on the police. Another is the provision of the Fifth Amendment that no person "shall be compelled 'in any criminal case' to be a witness against himself."

The invalidation of convictions based on confessions obtained by force and coercion is illustrated by many cases.[52] The words "in any criminal case" have not been confined to trials of the accused. They cover all investigations in which a witness gives testimony "which might tend to show that he himself had committed a crime." [53] Once a witness starts to talk about a matter, he is held to have waived his privilege of silence.[54] The corollary is that he need not testify to any phase of any matter that might furnish a link in the chain of evidence necessary for conviction of a crime.[55] The result is the closing of many doors to the prosecutor. The situation was remedied by Acts of Congress giving immunity to a witness for certain types of testimony. The controversy since then has turned on whether the immunity granted is coterminous with the

privilege.[56] In general, the decisions respect the privilege
against self-incrimination as a safeguard to the presumption of innocence accorded a defendant in a criminal trial.[57]
This privilege against self-incrimination marks an important difference between the Free Society and both fascism
and communism. Once government can make men talk,
ugly influences appear; the right of privacy is invaded; the
dignity of the individual is assaulted. This privilege, like
freedom of expression, is indispensable to the Free Society.

The Sixth Amendment requires a speedy public trial; it
says that the trial must be by an impartial jury and must
be held at the place where the crime was committed. These
provisions were inserted in response to the oppressive
practice of British colonial rulers who sometimes held men
for long periods without bringing them to trial. Sometimes
Americans were shipped abroad to be tried where the
colonial government was sure they would be convicted.
If they had been tried in their home country, the local
juries would have been very likely to acquit. The Sixth
Amendment prevents the prosecutor from shopping around
for a jurisdiction that seems favorable to the government.

This guarantee has its counterparts in state constitutions. Thus Tennessee in her Constitution grants "a speedy
public trial by an impartial jury of the county in which the
crime shall have been committed." [58] Once in the history
of that state (in the year 1962) a conscientious judge, after
a prolonged effort to impanel an impartial jury, finally
realized it was impossible. The sentiment of the entire
population of Hancock County was solidly ranged on
the side of the two defendants accused of murder. The
judge accordingly dismissed the indictment against them.[59]
This is an isolated instance where a constitutional guarantee goes astray. But it is a prized safeguard, for without

it prosecutors would be tempted to shop around for a city where the accused had no friends or where indeed the sentiment might be against him.

The Sixth Amendment also guarantees the accused a "public" trial. A secret trial would indeed be anathema to us. The advantages of a public trial over a secret one are obvious: a witness might testify secretly to things he would not dare say openly; lawyers and judges who could operate behind closed doors might take short cuts they would not dare take publicly; the community would not have a good measure of the manner in which justice was administered, if the public were excluded.

The constitutional requirement for a public trial did not arise out of any special grievance in English or American history. But the secret trial in France and Spain was known to us as a tyrannous practice of princes. It was therefore feared; and the common law consistently granted the right to a public trial.

The Court said in 1948: "Counsel have not cited and we have been unable to find a single instance of a criminal trial conducted *in camera* in any federal, state, or municipal court during the history of this country." [60]

The public trial can, of course, be an ominous affair. There have been times when a tense, crowded courtroom turned the trial into a theatrical performance, diverting it from a calm, dispassionate search for the truth. The hostility of the crowd inside the courtroom can indeed deprive the jury of its impartiality.

Boisterous and disorderly people are, of course, evicted from the courtroom. Some courts have gone further and allowed exclusion of a crowd of idle loafers whose presence at a trial is due to their morbid curiosity for indecent details. If an accused can show prejudice by reason of exclusion of members of the public, he gets a new trial. The exclusion of all of the bystanders, except the news reporters, has been soundly condemned.[61] But if the press is represented, if the defendant's lawyers, his witnesses, and some of his friends are present, and if a select group of the public (such as members of the bar) are admitted, the judge may, in exceptional situations, exclude the balance in the interest of justice.[62] A quiet, dignified courtroom is more likely to be a place of justice than one packed with people whose demeanor and attitude put the whole room on edge.

In federal courts and in most state courts, trials may not be televised or broadcast over the radio.[63] A few states let the trial judge in his discretion decide whether use of radio or television in the courtroom would prejudice the defendant. A complete ban is the only civilized alternative. Television cameras and radio microphones tend to make everyone an actor, including perhaps the judge. They make the trial a spectacle rather than a quiet, dignified proceeding where judge and jury are anxious to discover the truth and do justice.

The Sixth Amendment guarantees an accused in a criminal prosecution "the assistance of counsel for his defense" and "the right . . . to be confronted with the witnesses against him." The latter has echoes of the famous British trial of Sir Walter Raleigh.[64] The Raleigh trial was a notorious one, long remembered. It was one of the reasons why, prior to the Federal Constitution, some of the states wrote into their constitutions provisions giving an accused in a criminal trial the right to be confronted with the witnesses against him.

One of the main features of the American legal system is the jury trial. It is guaranteed by the Seventh Amendment in all criminal trials and in civil suits where the value in controversy exceeds $20. The right to trial by jury is deep in American tradition, whether life, liberty, or property is at stake. One of the complaints against the King of England in our Declaration of Independence was that he had deprived the colonists "in many cases of the benefits of trial by jury."

A jury reflects the attitudes and mores of the community from which it is drawn. It convenes only for the day and does justice according to its lights. The group of twelve, who are drawn to hear a case, makes the decision and melts away. It is not present the next day to be criticized. It is the one governmental agency that has no ambition. It is as human as the people who make it up. So it is sometimes the victim of passion. But it also takes the sharp edges off a law and uses conscience to ameliorate a hardship. Since it is of and from the community, it gives the law an acceptance which verdicts of judges could not do. The jury has a profound educational impact on the community. Through jury duty, the citizens come to know their government and its officials and better understand the problems of law enforcement.

A jury is supposed to represent a cross section of the community. While the United States is a nation of many races, the guarantee of a fair trial carries no promise that the defendant will have a member of his own race on the jury that tries him.[65] It is not their absence from the panel that is fatal. The fatal circumstance is discrimination. This protection of the jury system extends to the grand jury that makes the charge against the defendant as well as to the petit jury that tries him.[66]

Members of a race might, of course, be excluded for lack of qualifications, measured, for example, by literacy.

That is not the exclusion condemned by the Fourteenth Amendment. Nor does protection of the jury system against racial discrimination mean that each jury must be selected with an eye to proportional representation on the jury of all the races that live in a community.[67] The condemned discrimination is systematic exclusion of members of the race from the jury lists solely on account of race or color.[68] For example, where literate members of the race reside in the county but the jury lists have no members of that race on it year after year, a *prima facie* showing of discrimination is made out. For it will not be presumed that chance or accident was the cause of their continuous omission.[69] "When a jury selection plan, whatever it is, operates in such way as always to result in the complete and long-continued exclusion of any representative at all from a large group of Negroes, or any other racial group, indictments and verdicts returned against them by juries thus selected cannot stand." [70]

This constitutional rule has been applied most often in cases involving trials of Negroes. But it is not designed for their benefit alone. It extends as well to other racial groups; and it was applied where one of Mexican ancestry was convicted of murder and sentenced to life. It was shown that Americans of Mexican ancestry were systematically discriminated against in drawing grand juries and petit juries in this particular county. The conviction of the Mexican was therefore set aside, the Court saying:

> Throughout our history differences in race and color have defined easily identifiable groups which have at times required the aid of the courts in securing equal treatment under the laws. But community prejudices are not static, and from time to time other differences from

the community norm may define other groups which need the same protection. Whether such a group exists within a community is a question of fact. When the existence of a distinct class is demonstrated, and it is further shown that the laws, as written or as applied, single out that class for different treatment not based on some reasonable classification, the guarantees of the Constitution have been violated.[71]

As already noted, at the end of the Civil War, Amendments to the Constitution were adopted. The Thirteenth Amendment abolished slavery; the Fifteenth Amendment provided that the rights of citizens of the United States to vote shall not be denied or abridged either by the United States or any state on account of race, color, or previous condition of servitude; and the Fourteenth Amendment, among other things, provided for equal protection of the laws. It is around equal protection that perhaps the greatest controversies have turned.

One of the most offensive discriminations that Iraqis have known was imposed by the British after they took command of the country when the Ottoman Empire collapsed at the end of World War I. There were, and still are, many tribes in Iraq. Some are along the eastern and western borders in the south; others are in the north. These tribes were troublesome to the British. In an endeavor to control them, the British promulgated codes that put much harsher penalties on a member of a tribe than on other Iraqis for the *same* offense.[72] A tribal member who committed manslaughter could be sentenced to death; an Iraqi guilty of the same offense—indeed one who participated in the same crime—would never be executed. He might only be fined or at the most imprisoned. This discrimination was perpetuated by the Iraqi government that got its independence from the British. It was one festering factor that led to the *coup d'état* of 1958 when the King, the Crown Prince, and Nuri Said were assassinated.

The feeling of inequality before the law under colonial regimes has burned itself deeply into the consciousness of every subject people. And most of the constitutions of the newly emerged nations contain provisions that are designed to assure that the laws are administered equally among all the people. What is "equal protection"? Can some people be required to pay taxes at a higher rate than others? Do all burdens of government have to be distributed with an equal hand among all classes?

The problem of "equal protection" was stated thus: "The problems of government are practical ones and may justify, if they do not require, rough accommodations— illogical, it may be, and unscientific. . . . What is best is not always discernible; the wisdom of any choice may be disputed or condemned. Mere errors of government are not subject to our judicial review." [73]

When one draws a line, he makes a distinction that may be fair in most cases, yet arbitrary in some. A line drawn with reference to the average case on each side of the line may seem capricious when cases close to the line are considered. If that inequality cannot be tolerated, then the legislative branch is under heavy shackles. For one chief task of the lawmaker is to make classifications: graduating taxes according to income, regulating business according to size, protecting people according to age, requiring special health regulations for particular communities, reserving certain lands for specified purposes, restricting land holdings to maximum acreages, requiring some equipment to have safety devices, barring trucks of specified weights from the highways, and so on.

The equality of women commonly raises special problems. Yet to state a difference in sex is to state a classification that legislatures can make for some purposes. Hours of labor for women can be set with a view to the special requirements of the sex.[74] So may minimum wages.[75] The Court has even held that the State may ban bartending by women, since the legislature may have the allowable judgment that bartending by women gives rise "to moral and social problems" needing preventive measures.[76]

It was held that sterilization of imbeciles was permissible to prevent the perpetuation of those socially unfit and harmful people.[77] But when a sterilization law was applied to those who robbed banks from the outside, but not to those who raided them from within, the Court invalidated the law as denying equal protection. "When the law lays an unequal hand on those who have committed intrinsically the same quality of offense and sterilizes one and not the other, it has made as invidious a discrimination as if it had selected a particular race or nationality for oppressive treatment." [78]

Though no invidious discrimination appears on the face of the law, one may in practice exist. "Though the law itself be fair on its face and impartial in appearance, yet, if it is applied and administered by public authority with an evil eye and an unequal hand, so as practically to make unjust and illegal discriminations between persons in similar circumstances, material to their rights, the denial of equal justice is still within the prohibition of the Constitution." That case involved an ordinance of San Francisco, requiring a license to conduct a laundry business. Petitioner was a Chinese, long in the laundry business. He showed that this ordinance, which on its face was fair and applicable to all people, was in practice applied so as to exclude Chinese from the laundry business. The city could not, consistently with the Equal Protection Clause of the Fourteenth Amendment, have made that classification in the ordinance itself. Neither could the agency administering the ordinance apply it "with a mind so unequal and oppressive as to amount to a practical denial" of equal protection of the laws.[79]

Racial discrimination usually is the most pernicious of all and the easiest to detect. Most classifications based on race reflect an aim to suppress a people, or deny them benefits which other members of the community enjoy. The Soviet philosophy sounded noble: "From each according to his ability; to each according to his *need.*" But that was changed in practice: "From each according to his ability; to each according to his *deed.*" At once a vicious inequality entered the system. Moreover, in Russia, a Moslem who goes to his mosque regularly is penalized by not being promoted. If a man wants to get ahead in Russia, he should stay away from church. Racial minorities in the Soviet Union suffer discrimination. In Turkmenistan, Uzbekistan, Tadzhikistan, and Kazakhistan, the schools are segregated. The Russian gets 130 per cent of the salary of the Uzbek or other minority, even though he is doing the same work and exercising the same degree of skill. A Jew must have his race stamped on his identification paper.

In 1896, the Supreme Court sanctioned as constitutional the segregation of the white and colored races [80] on railroad cars. The rule announced set the pattern for the treatment of the Negro race. The rule was applied (not in all States but in quite a number of them) to all public facilities, as well as to railroads. It was extended also to community activities, including public schools.

The rule of *Plessy* v. *Ferguson* was the "separate but equal" doctrine. The races could be segregated, provided the facilities afforded one race were equal to the facilities afforded the other race. That is to say, Negroes could be put in a separate railroad car, a separate restaurant, a separate park, a separate school, provided the car, restaurant, park, or school separately provided was equal to the one reserved for whites.

This idea of segregation of races was embedded in community developments through the use of restrictive covenants. An area of a community was set aside exclusively for one race or another, and restrictive covenants were written into the deeds of title by which the grantee promised, for example, not to sell to anyone but a member of the Caucasian race. These restrictive covenants helped build segregated communities.

It was held that a city ordinance that forbade colored people from occupying houses in a zone reserved for whites was unconstitutional.[81] A city ordinance has all the compulsion of law; it is therefore state action within the meaning of the Fourteenth Amendment.

How about private arrangements? Is a covenant in a deed that restricts the sale of the property to members of a particular race valid? If the parties conform to the covenant without the compulsion of a state law, there is no state action that brings the Fourteenth Amendment into play. But suppose one does not comply with the covenant. Suppose he threatens to break it and a neighbor goes into court to enjoin the breach. May a court issue an injunction without violating the Fourteenth Amendment? The

Court held that judicial enforcement of these restrictive covenants through issuance of an injunction would be state action within the meaning of that Amendment.[82] The action of state courts and state judicial officers is as much state action as actions of the legislative branch or of the executive. The Fourteenth Amendment condemns all state action denying equal protection of the laws, whatever department of government is implicated.

A subsequent case involved a restrictive covenant on residential property. Only damages were sought when the covenant was broken. But that suit was also held to be barred by the Fourteenth Amendment. The Court refused to distinguish between an action to enjoin and an action for damages, saying: "To compel respondent to respond in damages would be for the State to punish her for her failure to perform her covenant to continue to discriminate against non-Caucasians in the use of her property. The result of that sanction by the State would be to encourage the use of restrictive covenants. To that extent, the State would act to put its sanction behind the covenants." [83]

The question of segregation in public schools was slow in coming to a head. But it finally was ripe for decision in 1954. Between 1896, the date of *Plessy* v. *Ferguson,* and 1954 there had been much litigation over the "separate but equal" doctrine. The Court had made clear over and again that segregation was permissible only if the facilities accorded Negroes were in fact equal to those accorded whites.

A State that had no law school for Negroes was under a duty to admit a qualified Negro student into its law school run for whites. The Court said: "The question here is not of a duty of the State to supply legal training, or of the

quality of the training which it does supply, but of its duty
when it provides such training to furnish it to the residents
of the State upon the basis of an equality of right. By the
operation of the laws of Missouri a privilege has been
created for white law students which is denied to Negroes
by reason of their race. The white resident is afforded
legal education within the State; the Negro resident having
the same qualifications is refused it there and must go
outside the State to obtain it. That is a denial of the equality of legal right to the enjoyment of the privilege which
the State has set up, and the provision for the payment of
tuition fees in another State does not remove the discrimination." [84]

One State provided a separate law school for Negroes.
But on showing that the school was not substantially equal
to the law school reserved for whites, the Court held that
a Negro candidate should be admitted into the latter
school.[85]

A Negro graduate student, though admitted to a white
school, was assigned to a row in class that was set aside
for Negroes, to a special table in the library, and to a
special table in the cafeteria. The Court held this segregation unconstitutional under the Fourteenth Amendment,
saying: "There is a vast difference—a Constitutional difference—between restrictions imposed by the State which
prohibit the intellectual commingling of students, and the
refusal of individuals to commingle where the State presents no such bar. . . . The removal of the State restrictions will not necessarily abate individual and group
predilections, prejudices and choices. But at the very least,
the state will not be depriving appellant of the opportunity
to secure acceptance by his fellow students on his own
merits." [86]

At last, the "separate but equal" doctrine itself was challenged. It was argued that, though the separate facilities were equal one to the other, segregation was *per se* unconstitutional. The question was squarely presented in 1954. A unanimous Court held the "separate but equal" doctrine unconstitutional, saying:

> Today, education is perhaps the most important function of state and local governments. Compulsory school attendance laws and the great expenditures for education both demonstrate our recognition of the importance of education to our democratic society. It is required in the performance of our most basic public responsibilities, even service in the armed forces. It is the very foundation of good citizenship. Today it is a principal instrument in awakening the child to cultural values, in preparing him for later professional training, and in helping him to adjust normally to his environment. In these days, it is doubtful that any child may reasonably be expected to succeed in life if he is denied the opportunity of an education. Such an opportunity, where the state has undertaken to provide it, is a right which must be made available to all on equal terms.[87]

In a companion case from the District of Columbia, which is a federal enclave, the Court reached the same result. That ruling was made in spite of the fact that the Fifth Amendment, which is applicable to the federal government, has no Equal Protection Clause. But racial discrimination, said the Court, may be so invidious as to violate the Due Process Clause of that Amendment. "Segregation in public education is not reasonably related to any proper governmental objective, and thus it imposes on Negro children of the District of Columbia a burden that constitutes an arbitrary deprivation of their liberty in violation of the Due Process Clause." [88]

Since the 1954 decision, progress has been made. Many public educational institutions formerly open only to white students in the southern states have adopted a non-discriminatory admission policy. So far as southern colleges and universities are concerned, a majority had complied to some degree with the *Brown* decision by the beginning of the 1960s. Less progress had been made in the elementary schools. Yet desegregation has been rather quickly achieved in some areas. All public schools in the District of Columbia, Maryland, and Delaware have been desegregated. Many other pockets of segregated schools have been eliminated.

The legal principle which the 1954 decision first articulated has, in succeeding years, been applied broadly. The States have long operated, for the benefit of the public, parks and beaches, pools and athletic facilities such as golf courses, or cultural facilities such as theatres. In 1955 the Supreme Court affirmed a holding that Negroes could not be denied relief "against the enforcement of racial segregation in the enjoyment of public beaches and bathhouses maintained by the public authorities of the State of Maryland." [89] On the same day that this decision was handed down, the Court reversed a decision wherein the lower court had held that Negroes would have to be satisfied with "separate but equal" access to a municipal golf course in Atlanta, Georgia.[90] And in 1961 it was held that a state could not avoid its responsibilities to provide equal protection of the laws through the device of a lease to a private person.[91] At times criminal statutes covering "disorderly conduct" or "disturbing the peace" are used as devices for enforcing a system of segregation against a

minority race. But the courts look through the sham and
set aside convictions where there is no evidence to support
the criminal charge.[92]

The thrust of the principle of the *Brown* case has been
felt in numerous ways. Many states *required* those offer-
ing public facilities or services of various kinds to discriminate. These requirements have crumbled. The Supreme Court struck down legally required segregation of
local buses in Montgomery, Alabama.[93] It affirmed the
overturning of a state statute that forbade Negroes and
Caucasians to engage in a prize fight.[94]

The great arteries of interstate commerce have been
affirmatively cleared of segregation. Acting under its en-
abling statutes, the Interstate Commerce Commission has
forbidden segregation on interstate trains and buses and in
terminals. This prohibition of segregation was extended to
restaurants located along an interstate bus route which
are an "integral part of . . . transportation." [95] Discrimination is also outlawed, by federal statute, as to airlines.[96]

By 1962 the proposition had become so well settled that
the Court said that one who questioned it was raising a
frivolous question.[97]

Affirmative federal action has abolished segregation in
the armed services. In 1948, President Truman promulgated an executive order ending segregation in each
branch.[98] By 1955, the Department of Defense reported
full implementation of that order.[99]

There is much yet to be done before the philosophy of
the *Brown* decision is fully reflected in American life, but
great progress has been made.

While social discrimination on the part of government
is still in vogue in some areas, the law in America is
against the practice. The Constitution proclaims the prin-

ciple of equality—equality for the man who disagrees with government, as well as for the party member; equality for a man no matter his religion; equality for a man no matter his race.

The American multi-racial communities have had internal conflicts and stresses arising from racial tensions and animosities. Sometimes those conflicts have flared up into ugly episodes. Usually they have been amicably settled. They have always been settled peacefully when we have been true to the principle of equality stated in the Declaration of Independence.

Wherever equality is the theme, men live together in peace. Wherever inequality is the practice, grievances and complaints fester. That is as true of Europe, Asia, Africa, and South America as it is of the United States. Equality among men of all creeds, nationalities, and colors is the great curative of social ills. No one segment of society can long be set apart in a ghetto of second- or third-class citizenship. Once that happens, a divisive influence is at work, one that will sooner or later tear the community apart.

As an eighteenth-century American, Joel Barlow, said concerning the theme that all men are equal in their rights: "This point once settled, everything is settled. . . . Banish the mysticism of inequality and you banish almost all the evils attendant on human nature." [100]

Gandhi spoke eloquently of the problem when he pleaded for abolition of the caste of the Untouchables: "We must not throw a few miserable schools at them: we must not adopt the air of superiority towards them. We must treat them as our blood brothers as they are in fact. We must return to them the inheritance of which we have robbed them. And this must not be the act of a few English-knowing reformers merely, but it must be a conscious voluntary effort on the part of the masses." [101]

Dr. Sarvepalli Radhakrishnan, now the President of India, said: "Only differents can unite on the basis of unity of all alike, reality residing in each individual and the joy of fulfillment when truth is attained." [102]

Equal protection under the law is the most important single principle that any nation can take as its ideal. Those who practice it have a strength and unity that other nations lack. Those who practice it give to each minority a sense of belonging. A sense of belonging is, perhaps, the most important community attitude a people can have. Where there is a sense of belonging, there are ties of loyalty and devotion that no strains of politics can ever sever or destroy.

All men of course are not equal in talents or abilities. But once all men are treated equally by government and afforded equal opportunities for preferment and advancement, society undergoes a transformation. A new aristocracy emerges—not an aristocracy of family, wealth, race, or religion, but an *aristocracy of talent*. An *aristocracy of talent* that draws from all the roots of the community is indeed the distinguishing mark of democracy.

Gandhi once called for an India without "race hatred." "Let that be our nationalism," said Gandhi. That was also the call of Abraham Lincoln and Franklin D. Roosevelt. A nation without race hatred is singularly strong in spirit.

The ideal that Gandhi set for his nation and that Lincoln and Roosevelt set for America is the ideal that is now set for the new world community.

The General Assembly of the United Nations in the Universal Declaration of Human Rights proclaimed the principle of equality for all peoples: "Everyone is entitled to all the rights and freedoms set forth in this Declaration, without distinction of any kind, such as race, colour, sex, language, religion, political or other opinion, national or social origin, property, birth or other status." [103]

This equality includes the abolition of slavery; equal treatment before the law; the right to marry across racial, national, or religious lines; the right of equality of access to public service; the right to equal pay for equal work.

Universal suffrage is proclaimed; and freedom of thought, conscience, and religion, freedom of opinion and expression are guaranteed by the Declaration.

It does, indeed, raise the sights of all nations to renewed efforts to reach the ideal of the brotherhood of man proclaimed by all the great religions of the world.

Yet in spite of all declarations the human race has gained more in knowledge than in wisdom over the centuries. Not many nations can say today what Pericles said in 431 B.C.:

> . . . this our form, as committed not to the few, but to the whole body of the people, is called a democracy. How different soever in a private capacity, we all enjoy the same general equality our laws are fitted to preserve; and superior honors just as we excel. The public administration is not confined to a particular family, but is attainable only by merit. Poverty is not a hindrance, since whoever is able to serve his country meets with no obstacle to preferment from his first obscurity. The offices of the State we go through without obstructions from one another; and live together in the mutual endearments of private life without suspicions.[104]

II

EXECUTIVE vs. LEGISLATIVE vs. JUDICIAL

> *"The accumulation of all powers, legislative, executive, and judiciary, in the same hands, whether of one, a few, or many, and whether hereditary, self-appointed, or elective, may justly be pronounced the very definition of tyranny."*
> —JAMES MADISON

LIBERTY has been greatly curtailed when all the powers of government are in one person's hands. That is true whether the person be an individual, a church, an oligarchy, a politburo, or an army. It is true whether that person represents one class, one ideology, one religion, or one race. The experience of centuries is that one indispensable requirement of a Free Society is a division of power; and in the United States the division is made into three parts. That division was first made by Aristotle.[1]

The principle of the separation of powers was contained in the Declaration of Rights in the Massachusetts Constitution of 1780: "In the government of this commonwealth, the legislative department shall never exercise the executive and judicial powers, or either of them; the executive shall never exercise the legislative and judicial

53

powers, or either of them; the judicial shall never exercise the legislative and executive powers, or either of them: to the end it may be a government of laws and not of men." [2]

Six of the original states explicitly affirmed the doctrine of the separation of powers. Today the theory is formally announced in about forty state constitutions. The other states make no such formal declaration; nor does the Constitution of the United States. Yet the same result is reached because these other states' constitutions, as the federal constitution, create three departments of government, vesting the executive power in one, the legislative power in another, and the judicial power in a third.

James Madison stated the philosophy behind this system: ". . . the great security against a gradual concentration of the several powers in the same department, consists in giving to those who administer each department the necessary constitutional means and personal motives to resist encroachments of the others. . . . It may be a reflection on human nature, that such devices should be necessary to control the abuses of government. But what is government itself, but the greatest of all reflections on human nature? If men were angels, no government would be necessary." [3]

John Adams said, "A legislative, an executive, and a judicial power comprehend the whole of what is meant and understood by government. It is by balancing each of these powers against the other two, that the efforts in human nature towards tyranny can alone be checked and restrained, and any freedom preserved in the Constitution." [4]

Montesquieu went so far as to say that "when the legislative and executive powers are united in the same person or in the same body of magistracy, there can be no liberty." [5]

That theory would make impossible a parliamentary system such as England, Australia, and India use. Yet their cabinet systems work well. In the United States, however, a cabinet system is not possible, because the Constitution provides: "No person holding any office under the United States shall be a member of either House during his continuance in office." [6]

It was the theory of the Framers that a republican form of government, not a democracy, was preferable. "In a democracy, where a multitude of people exercise in person the legislative functions, and are continually exposed, by their incapacity for regular deliberation and concerted measures, to the ambitious intrigues of their executive magistrates, tyranny may well be apprehended, on some favorable emergency, to start up in the same quarter." [7]

The Executive Power

The executive power is vested in the President who has a term of four years; but no one may be elected to the office more than twice. The President is the ceremonial head of the nation. He represents the nation as does no other single individual. When he goes abroad, he *is* the United States. When he entertains the heads of other nations, he is also a host acting for all the American people. The President is the initiator of policies. This function is not exclusively his, because the Congress on its own may (and often does) propose legislation. Yet the President is pre-eminently the one to shape and fashion policy, changing it from one direction to another, giving existing policy new impetus, or deciding (as a few Presidents have done) that the less a government does, the better it is. While the President can recommend legislation, only a member of Congress can introduce a bill that embodies a proposed law.

The President reports to Congress on the state of the Union, and he recommends those laws that he considers expedient and necessary. He has the power to convene Congress in a special session; and if the two Houses cannot agree on adjournment, he may adjourn them to such a time as he deems proper. The President has occasionally convened Congress into a special session. That was, for example, done by Roosevelt on March 5, 1933, the day after his First Inaugural when the nation seemed to be on the brink of economic disaster. The President's authority to adjourn Congress has never been exercised.

The President fashions policies not only by his appeals to the people and by his influence with legislators. He also fashions policy by his appointment power: the judicious exercise of this power gives him the opportunity to select like-minded people who will carry forward his program. He chooses, of course, the members of his Cabinet. He names ambassadors, ministers, and consuls to represent the country abroad. He nominates federal judges and many other public officials.

His control, of course, is not unlimited. None of these appointments is valid unless confirmed by the Senate, and nominations of judges, as well as administrators, have sometimes been rejected. Even if the President should make an appointment while Congress is not in session, such an appointment would expire before the end of the next session, unless confirmed.

A great number of public offices, however, may be filled by the President alone or by the department heads, or by the courts, when Congress so delegates. Positions in the lower levels of the hierarchy are mostly named by department heads, and the vast majority of them are protected in tenure by the Civil Service Act, which in origin goes back to 1883. Because the President or his cabinet officers control the top-level policy-making positions, he is able to steer this large bureaucracy as he wishes.

The officials named by the President or by his Cabinet, alone, may be removed at will, unless they are protected in tenure by Civil Service. But those who must be confirmed by the Senate have a special immunity. They are more than mere executive officers, doing the will of the President. They also enforce laws passed by Congress; they regulate various segments of American life; and they adjudicate controversies. They cannot be removed by the President unless an Act of Congress makes their tenure terminable in that manner. A good reason for such a distinction can be seen in the 1958 case in which the Court held unlawful the attempted removal by Eisenhower of a Truman appointee to the War Claims Commission. The Court said: "If, as one must take for granted, the War Claims Act precluded the President from influencing the Commission in passing on a particular claim, *a fortiori* must it be inferred that Congress did not wish to have hang over the Commission the Damocles sword of removal by the President for no reason other than that he preferred to have on that Commission men of his own choosing." [8]

Congress at times makes officers, named by the President and confirmed by the Senate, removable by the President. Such is the case of the civilian judges who make up the Court of Military Appeals and whose tenure, unless earlier terminated by the President, is fifteen years. They

may be removed on notice and hearing "for neglect of
duty or malfeasance in office, or for mental or physical
disability, but for no other cause." [9]

It is the role of the President to execute the laws as
well as to formulate policies to be embodied in new laws
or in new projects under existing laws. The question
whether certain action by the President constitutes the
execution of existing laws or the making of new laws
sometimes gives rise to heated controversies.

Thus, when President Truman in 1952 took over the
steel mills of the nation in an effort to settle a strike, the
steel companies sought a court order prohibiting the President from seizing the mills. The President had seized
them as a result of a labor dispute which threatened steel
production, vital to the national defense during the Korean
War. The steel companies charged that the seizure was
not authorized by any Act of Congress and therefore was
invalid. In upholding that contention, the Court stated
that the function of the President is to see that the laws
are faithfully executed; that the function of Congress is to
make the laws. It is to Congress that the legislative power
has been entrusted by the Constitution. "The founders of
this Nation," said the Court, "entrusted the lawmaking
power to the Congress alone in both good and bad
times." [10] The seizure was accordingly invalid, since Congress had not authorized it.

The conduct of foreign relations is largely committed
to the President, who determines what countries should be
recognized, and who, subject to Senate confirmation,
should represent the nation overseas. Moreover, the Constitution grants the President "power, by and with the
Advice and Consent of the Senate, to make Treaties, provided two-thirds of the Senators present concur." [11]

But a custom early developed whereby the President on his own and without participation by the Senate entered into certain arrangements with other nations "in the nature of treaties." [12] These were in the beginning international postal agreements. Later Presidents made various kinds of trade agreements with foreign nations.[13] President Roosevelt, when he recognized Soviet Russia, agreed to the Litvinov Assignment; and its terms for settlement of claims of American nationals against Russia and Russian companies were sustained over and against the claim of New York State that the terms of this assignment were contrary to her policies.[14] For that kind of executive agreement is part and parcel of the act of recognition of a foreign government—a prerogative vested exclusively in the President.

While the power of the President to make agreements "in the nature of treaties" and without the advice and consent of the Senate is established, the lines are not clear. The pressure for a constitutional amendment to clarify it has been much discussed. The problem has been solved by practical considerations which lead the President to submit international agreements to the Senate for approval except as they are intertwined with the recognition of foreign nations, with the performance of his special duties as Commander-in-Chief, or are administrative in character.[15] In large measure Congress has solved the problem by passing laws which grant the President broad powers to deal with sensitive areas in foreign affairs. The Supreme Court commented: "Practically every volume of the United States Statutes contains one or more acts or joint resolutions of Congress authorizing action by the President in respect of subjects affecting foreign relations, which either leave the exercise of the power to his unrestricted judgment, or provide a standard far more general than that which has always been considered requisite with regard to domestic affairs." [16]

The President has long had authority under various Acts of Congress to reduce or adjust tariffs.[17] It is now realized that he must have even broader powers so as to be able to negotiate on a broad basis for mutual tariff reductions with other nations and make the necessary accommodations with the new nations that are emerging, as well as with the common markets.[18]

Private rights often flow from treaties, which means that controversies arise in which the courts are necessarily implicated. But the question whether a particular treaty has survived a war between two nations turns essentially on the policies formulated and adopted by the political departments of the government. The courts do not determine independently whether a treaty has survived; they merely ascertain what the policy of the political departments in respect to the survival of treaties has been.[19]

The power to conduct foreign affairs includes, as already indicated, the power to recognize a particular regime as the *de jure* or *de facto* sovereign of another nation. When the political branches of government have spoken, the propriety of that political action is not open to judicial inquiry or decision.[20]

Whether dominion over new territory has been acquired by discovery and occupation, by cession, or by conquest is also a question for the political departments of government, not for the judiciary.[21]

Recognition or non-recognition of another nation is a political act that often has repercussions in litigation. So long as the political departments of the United States recognize a foreign government, the courts of the United

States will not entertain litigation opposed to that policy. Texas broke away from Mexico. While the treaty of amity and friendship with Mexico was still in force, some American citizens entered into a contract which was designed to help Texas finance its revolution. Suit was brought for specific performance of the contract. The bill was dismissed, since the contract was in contravention of the policy of the political departments.[22]

If the act of recognition of a foreign power includes a policy of providing for the settlement or payment of certain claims, that policy is binding on the judiciary.[23] The extent to which our courts have gone in sustaining the foreign policy set by the executive department is illustrated by the exemptions from litigation which the courts have traditionally accorded to ships and vessels of a foreign country. In one such case, the Supreme Court held that "the judicial seizure of the vessel of a friendly foreign state is so serious a challenge to its dignity, and may so affect our friendly relations with it, that courts are required to accept and follow the executive determination that the vessel is immune." [24]

The salaries of the President and other executive officers and other expenses of the executive department must be voted by Congress; but the salary of the President may neither be increased nor decreased during his term.

The President has the power of pardon or reprieve for federal offenses, except in cases of impeachment. His power to grant pardons may not be qualified by Congress. After the Civil War, Congress refused standing to those who had rebelled against the nation to pursue claims against the United States, even though the claimants had been pardoned by the President. The Court said: "To the executive alone is intrusted the power of pardon; and it is granted without limit. Pardon includes amnesty. It blots out the offence pardoned and removes all its penal consequences. It may be granted on conditions." [25]

The President is Commander-in-Chief of the Army and Navy. As such, his office marks the victorious result of a long effort to make the civilian authority supreme over the military. Younger nations have suffered from a lack of this tradition. When Ayub in Pakistan, Ne Win in Burma and Chung Hee Park in South Korea took control from the civilian authority by force, they turned the clock backward. Long before the American Revolution, it was established in England that the army was subordinate to the civilian authority and that the laws for the government of the armed forces were written by the civilian authority.

The American attitude toward the military was well stated by Samuel Adams in 1768, who in protest to the stationing of a British army in Boston said:

> . . . let us then assert & maintain the honor—the dignity of free citizens, and place the military where all other men are, and where they always ought & always will be plac'd in every free country, at the foot of the common law of the land. To submit to the civil magistrate in the legal exercise of power is forever the part of a good subject; and to answer the watchmen of the town in the night may be the part of a good citizen, as well as to afford them all necessary countenance and support. But, to be called to account by a common soldier, or any soldier, is a badge of slavery which none but a slave will wear.[26]

There are many ways in which the civilian authority is made superior to the military. By law, the Secretaries in charge of the various branches of the Armed Services must be civilians—a requirement that Congress by a special Act waived to allow General George C. Marshall to serve in the Cabinet as Secretary of Defense. And in the Uniform Code of Military Justice, enacted in 1950, a court composed of civilians and designated as a Court of Military Appeals was made the agency of final review of questions of law arising in cases from courts-martial.[27] Moreover, Congress has provided in the Selective Service Acts that the hand of the Army court-martial does not reach the draftee until and unless he is "actually inducted" into the Army; for failure or refusal to be inducted, he is triable not by the military but by the civil courts.[28] Before the soldier is actually in the Armed Services the civilian authority retains jurisdiction over him to the exclusion of the military; and after he is in, the civilian court has the final review over the action of the military authorities in disciplining or punishing him.

Three episodes illustrate the deep-seated reluctance of this nation to surrender power to the military establishment.

First, our courts-martial had no jurisdiction to try soldiers for murders committed by them until Congress, in 1863, enacted a statute conferring such jurisdiction. Prior to that time, if a soldier committed murder, only state courts had jurisdiction over the offense. The American tradition has long been hostile "to any interference by the military with the regular administration of justice in the civil courts." [29]

Second, civilian witnesses before courts-martial could not be forced to testify prior to 1901. In that year Congress passed a law making it their duty to testify. But

Congress did not give the power to the military to punish them for refusing. Rather, it made them punishable in the civil courts. And that is the law today.

Third, while civil courts (apart from the Court of Military Appeals) do not sit in review of military tribunals, civil courts do entertain the writ of *habeas corpus* by which the jurisdiction of the military tribunal can be challenged. The military exceed their jurisdiction when they undertake to try civilians in time of peace; and even in time of war military jurisdiction over civilians is extremely limited. Courts-martial also exceed their jurisdiction when they deprive an accused of a constitutional right. For example, a denial of an opportunity to the accused to tender the defense of insanity would be a denial of due process which could be challenged by *habeas corpus*.[30] *Habeas corpus* is also available where punishment is imposed for an act not made illegal by Congress.

The President as Commander-in-Chief can, and sometimes does, send federal troops to put down insurrections or riots. While that power is entrusted to him alone, he is subject to a rule of law in those activities that touch the life, liberty, or property of the individual.

The instances where the President has sent federal troops into the States to perform various missions have been numerous.[31] The purpose usually has been to protect federal property or to enforce a federal court decree or other law when it was felt that local enforcement machinery had broken down. In general, these were instances where military power was invoked to support, rather than to displace, the civilian authority.

The fact that troops must be called out to suppress insurrections or to enforce a court decree or to guard against invasion does not mean that a single function of the civil authorities need be disturbed. The American tradition has been just the reverse. In the Whiskey Rebellion of 1794, Washington instructed the commander of the troops to see to it that the laws were enforced and to turn over any insurgents to the civil courts for trial. The objects of the military force were stated to be twofold:

1. To overcome any armed opposition which may exist.
2. To countenance and support the civil officers in the means of executing the law.[32]

Even in time of war the power of the military authority is limited, as already noted.

The Constitution leaves to the military "cases arising in the land or naval forces." [33] Military courts sit in those cases pursuant to the Code of Military Justice by which Congress has prescribed the procedure that must be followed. Many of the safeguards in our Bill of Rights are not applicable to military trials: there is no need for a grand jury to return an indictment; the accused does not get the benefit of a jury trial; military officers who sit as judges often have no foundation in the law and no training in the democratic traditions of law administration.

As already indicated, the military have a very limited authority over civilians. A civilian who commits treason can be tried only by a civilian court. Civilians who are attached to the Army or Navy fall in a different category. Yet the class of civilians who can be tried by military courts even in time *of war* is small.

Military trials of civilians in times *of peace* are not possible under the American system. Once a soldier is discharged from the armed service he cannot be arrested by the military and tried for a crime committed when he was a soldier.[34] Members of the families of soldiers and sailors serving overseas cannot be tried by the military for their overseas crimes.[35] A civilian attached to the Armed Services, doing work for them, and stationed overseas likewise may not be tried for his overseas crimes by military courts.[36] Those who assassinated Lincoln were tried by a military commission and executed. But that trial was plainly unconstitutional, for later the Supreme Court held that even *in war* a civilian is entitled to be tried by a civil court.[37] Battles may close some courts. But if the civil courts are open in a theatre of war, they must try civilians; the military is without power to do so.

A regime of martial law may be lawful in time of peace as well as in war. As the Court stated in 1849, ". . . a State may use its military power to put down an armed insurrection, too strong to be controlled by the civil authority. The power is essential to the existence of every government, essential to the preservation of order and free institutions, and is as necessary to the States of this Union as to any other government." [38]

Once martial law is established, the civil authority gives way to the military, to a degree. Searches and seizures may be made which would be beyond the authority of civilian officers. People may be killed in the actual clash of arms without liability. Suspects may be arrested. In other ways, as yet undefined, personal liberties may be impaired under martial law that would be denounced as violations of the Bill of Rights under a civilian regime. Even so, there are strict limits, as already noted. Arrests may be justified, but not detention. Those arrested must be turned over to the civil authorities for trial and punishment. The power to detain a citizen at the whim of the military would indeed give the military the authority to suspend the writ of *habeas corpus,* which, the Constitution says, may not be done "unless when in cases of rebellion or invasion the public safety may require it." [39] Lincoln suspended the writ in the Civil War and Congress ratified the action. The authority of the President to do it alone and without the support of Congress has never been decided.

As a distinguished authority on this subject has written, "Martial law prevents, but it does not punish." [40] If the insurrection or riot has closed the civil courts, it would be part of "the duty devolving upon the military" to open them, as the Supreme Court of Montana said.[41]

There are expressions of opinion in some of the early cases that the authority to decide whether conditions are sufficiently acute to justify the establishment of martial law belongs exclusively to the Chief Executive and that his decision is conclusive. But it is now established that the final voice of authority in determining the lawfulness of military actions is the judiciary, not the military, not the executive that authorizes the military to act, not the legislative branch that sanctions martial law.

"What are the allowable limits of military discretion, and whether or not they have been overstepped in a particular case, are judicial questions." That was the view of a unanimous court when it limited the power of a governor of a state to declare martial law during domestic troubles.

A federal court had set aside an order of the Railroad Commission of Texas which limited the production of oil from certain wells. The Governor declared martial law in the territory where these oil wells were located and ordered the state militia to limit the oil production as directed by the Railroad Commission. The lower federal court, in a suit to enjoin the Governor from pursuing that course, found that there had been no riot, tumult, or insurrection in Texas and that martial law had been illegally imposed. The Supreme Court sustained that finding, saying that "there was no military necessity which, from any point of view, could be taken to justify the action of the Governor in attempting to limit complainants' oil production, otherwise lawful. . . . There was no exigency which justified the Governor in attempting to enforce by executive or military order the restriction" [42] which the lower court had set aside.

There is no more important decision subjecting the military power to civilian authority. When the liberties of the citizens are involved, the judiciary has the final say on whether martial law is justified. Executive fiat is not enough.

One of the most extravagant applications of military authority, authorized by the President, was in Hawaii during World War II. Immediately following the attack on Pearl Harbor, the Governor of Hawaii undertook by proclamation to place the Territory under "martial law." He was authorized by the Organic Act to take this action "in case of rebellion or invasion, or imminent danger thereof, when the public safety requires it." But his action in that regard was to remain in effect only until the President could act. The President approved the Governor's action on December 9. The regime which was brought into being was a severe one. The Commanding General was authorized to exercise all the powers normally exercised by the Governor and by the judicial officers and employees of Hawaii. Pursuant to this authority the Commanding General established military courts to take the place of civil courts; and he forbade civil courts to summon jurors or witnesses or to try cases. A military government was installed in Hawaii with the Army exercising all legislative, executive, and judicial control. The story is grim. When the writ of *habeas corpus* was restored in 1943 there were many unseemly contests between the courts and the Army. The Army even undertook to prohibit judges from entertaining *habeas corpus* petitions. Thousands were convicted in these military courts and received sentences not authorized by the law of the land.[43]

When invasion of the Pacific Coast area by the Japanese in World War II seemed imminent, the military, acting pursuant to the authority of the President as Commander-in-Chief, established a curfew for all persons of Japanese ancestry, whether citizens or aliens,[44] and later excluded all such persons from the coastal area.[45] The power in time of war to take those extreme measures was sustained in decisions of questionable authority.

While those decisions are arguably right in not overruling the military on its appraisal of the likelihood that the Japanese army might land on the West Coast, they seem in retrospect to be wrong in letting the military remove those citizens via concentration centers. The constitutional power to place those who were removed in camps in the interior was never squarely ruled upon, though it was held that the military had been granted no such authority. Loyalty is not a matter of race or color. Even a person suspected of crime cannot be arrested, except on a warrant issued by a magistrate on a showing of probable cause. As earlier stated, preventive detention is allowed in many other nations, but it is inconsistent with the Fourth and Fifth Amendments of our Constitution. Those who commit acts of disloyalty may, of course, be arrested. But ancestry is no basis for an arrest or for detention.[46]

Experience in America and elsewhere proves that the military should be entrusted only with strictly military tasks. One reason is the nature of martial law as contrasted to civil administration. Martial law in time of peace is a regime to put down riots, rebellion, and insurrection. Martial law in time of war is a regime to help wage the war successfully. Martial law, however invoked, is the use of force rather than persuasion, the rule by military edict rather than by laws made by representatives of the people, the assertion of arbitrary power rather than the due process of law guaranteed by the Constitution. Martial law and civil liberty are, therefore, in conflict: a conflict which is irreconcilable.[47]

To repeat: The fact that it is necessary to call out the militia to quell a riot does not necessarily mean that the military have to take over all the functions of the police. The fact that some men need be arrested does not mean that the writ of *habeas corpus* need be suspended. The fact that manpower must be mobilized to meet impending invasion does not mean the courts need be closed. The fact that hostilities are imminent does not mean that newspapers must submit to censorship. The fact that saboteurs may be at large, who can be tried by the military, does not mean that the military should also try traffic violations, domestic relation disputes, automobile accident cases, and ordinary criminal cases.

The military, though still subordinate to the civilian authority, has increased its influence since World War II. Its influence has mounted as its budget has increased. Today that budget is over fifty billion dollars a year, an amount that is greater than the total income of the 600 million people under the Peking regime, if their average per capita income is generously estimated at $80 a year.

The fifty billion expended annually by the Pentagon is spent at home and distributed abroad in the form of foreign aid. From this position of power the military and the arms industry which has grown to supply it exercise control over foreign and domestic affairs in a way not envisioned by the Constitution.

The funds reach so many aspects of our life that none is unaffected. Those who benefit from these expenditures know their master's voice and tend to walk in conformity. The result is a deadening of criticism and concomitantly a tendency for people to think in military rather than in political terms, though the arrival of the nuclear age has made war more and more obsolete. President Eisenhower, in his Farewell Address, warned of these dangers:

> Our military organization today bears little relation to that known to any of my predecessors in peacetime— or, indeed, by the fighting men of World War II or Korea.
>
> Until the latest of our world conflicts, the United States had no armaments industry. American makers of plowshares could, with time and as required, make swords as well. . . .
>
> Now this conjunction of an immense military establishment and a large arms industry is new in the American experience. The total influence—economic, political, even spiritual—is felt in every city, every state house, every office of the Federal Government. . . . [W]e must not fail to comprehend . . . [the] grave implications. Our toil, resources and livelihood are all involved; so is the very structure of our society.

President Eisenhower, who knows the military mind

and who better than anyone in our age appreciates how limited it is, asked in his Farewell Address that the situation be redressed:

> In the councils of Government, we must guard against the acquisition of unwarranted influence, whether sought or unsought, by the military-industrial complex. The potential for the disastrous rise of misplaced power exists and will persist.
>
> We must never let the weight of this combination endanger our liberties or democratic processes. We should take nothing for granted. Only an alert and knowledgeable citizenry can compel the proper meaning of the huge industrial and military machinery of defense with our peaceful methods and goals, so that security and liberty may prosper together.

The growing influence of the Pentagon in American thinking is illustrative of how basic alterations in a constitutional scheme can be effected without a rewriting of the document.

The Congress may not investigate the President; it may not summon him. In defending himself against investigation by Congress every President has acted rightfully. In refusing to be investigated by Congress he defends popular sovereignty and the separation of powers.

Most Presidents—either during their term or after their retirement—have been asked by Congress for information or even asked to testify before Congressional Committees. Each President has felt that it was a perquisite of the office not to appear as a witness. In 1953 President Truman responded to a subpoena issued by a committee of the House as follows:

It must be obvious to you that if the doctrine of separation of powers and the independence of the Presidency is to have any validity at all, it must be equally applicable to a President after his term of office has expired when he is sought to be examined with respect to any acts occurring while he is President.

The doctrine would be shattered, and the President, contrary to our fundamental theory of constitutional government, would become a mere arm of the Legislative Branch of the Government if he would feel during his term of office that his every act might be subject to official inquiry and possible distortion for political purposes.

If your intention, however, is to inquire into any acts as a private individual either before or after my Presidency and unrelated to any acts as President, I shall be happy to appear.[48]

Congress of course can investigate the administration of laws by the executive department. But it may not investigate the President himself—except by impeachment.

That is the only way to oust him from office. Impeachment is voted by the House of Representatives. The Senators sit as the judges; and when the President is tried, the Chief Justice presides. No person can be convicted on impeachment "without the concurrence of two-thirds of the members present." Only one President has been impeached by the House and tried by the Senate. He was Andrew Johnson, who followed Lincoln. Johnson, like Lincoln, wanted to make a reconciliation with the southern states, not to wreak vengeance on them. One of his attorneys, William Groesbeck, addressed the Senate as follows:

He was eager for pacification. He thought that the war

was ended. The drums were all silent; the arsenals were all shut; the roar of the cannon had died away to the last reverberations; the armies were disbanded; not a single enemy confronted us in the field. Ah, he was too eager, too forgiving, too kind. The hand of conciliation was stretched out to him and he took it. It may be he should have put it away, but was it a crime to take it? Kindness, forgiveness a crime? Kindness a crime? Kindness is omnipotent for good, more powerful than gunpowder or cannon. Kindness is statesmanship. Kindness is the high statesmanship of heaven itself.[49]

Andrew Johnson was acquitted; and impeachment as a political weapon was cast aside, never to be used again. Had that impeachment succeeded, those blinded by partisan zeal would have had a powerful weapon with which to destroy the leader of the opposition.

Each President—from Washington to Kennedy—has deemed it to be in his prerogative not to disclose certain information to the legislative branch. Taft defended that principle, saying a President can keep information confidential "if he does not deem the disclosure of such information prudent or in the public interest." [50] Certainly much information must be kept secret; at least, the President might so believe. Defense items, the operations of diplomatic missions, the communications with our embassies or legations—these are sensitive matters. Moreover, employees of the executive branch are in a chain of command leading up to the President. If any of them can be summoned and interrogated as to how he advised his superior, what memoranda he wrote, what conversation he has had, a disruptive influence would be injected into the executive branch. Then the employee would look to Congress and not have undivided loyalty to his superior in the executive branch. That was the philosophy behind Eisenhower's directive in 1954 to the Secretary of Defense:

> Because it is essential to efficient and effective administration that employees of the Executive Branch be in a position to be completely candid in advising with each other on official matters, and because it is not in the public interest that any of their conversations or communications, or any documents or reproductions, concerning such advice be disclosed, you will instruct employees of your Department that in all of their appearances before the Subcommittee of the Senate Committee on Government Operations regarding the inquiry now before it they are not to testify to any such conversations or communications or to produce any such documents or reproductions. This principle must be maintained regardless of who would be benefitted by such disclosures.[51]

The bounds are impossible to describe with particularity. They rest in the discretion of the President and in the tolerance of Congress. As recently stated: ". . . on the whole, a good case can be made out for the proposition that the present imprecise situation is, in fact, reasonably satisfactory. Neither the executive nor the Congress is very sure of its rights, and both usually evince a tactful disposition not to push the assertion of their rights to abusive extremes. Of such is the system of checks and balances." [52]

Or as another scholar has put the matter: "The separation of powers, then, has a double aspect. First, it is intended to prevent the excessive concentration of power in a single branch of government. Second, it is designed to insure maximum operating efficiency. Where the two meet, there lies the problem of executive secrecy. Viewed from the first aspect, executive secrecy is a flaw in demo-

cratic philosophy: if we dread tyranny, we cannot tolerate
a president who keeps Congress and the people in ignorance of his acts. Viewed from the second aspect, executive
secrecy is an integral part of democratic philosophy. . . ." [53]

The American political creed has as its main ingredient
the sovereignty of goodwill. The three branches operate
with respect for each other's function. As a Senate Report
on the power of Congress to investigate recently said: "In
exercising its authority, Congress of necessity will be
guided by good judgment and expediency, giving due
consideration to the nature of the inquiry, the state of
public and international affairs, and the general welfare
of the country." [54]

Controversies frequently rage over what information
should be confidential and what should not be. An American who was among those responsible for making the
atomic bomb said, "The ultimate responsibility for our
nation's policy rests on its citizens and they can discharge
such responsibilities wisely only if they are informed." The
American people have received little information on the
amount, nature, and dangers of fall-out resulting from
Russian, French, English, and American testing of nuclear
bombs. This is an example of the dangers of excessive
classification of information as "secret." When lines are
drawn in the interests of the security of the nation, everything touching on nuclear activities and progress is apt to
be classified as "secret." The problem is not acute in communist lands. For there the politburo has the welfare of the
country in its exclusive possession. But in a republican
form of government, where the ultimate sovereignty lies
with the people, doubts concerning the advisability of
making information "secret" must always be resolved in

favor of publicity. For without knowledge the electorate cannot act intelligently.

Moreover, when individual rights are concerned, different considerations come into play. Can a person be convicted of a crime and yet not have access to the documents in the possession of the government on which the issue of guilt or innocence may turn? Can the Chief Executive or a Cabinet officer make those documents secret and not producible in court? If so, is it Due Process to send a man to prison or to death where innocence might be established or guilt put in doubt were the documents produced? The answer is "no." The matter has been extensively litigated.[55] Congress finally legislated concerning the manner in which a "statement or report" of the United States that is used in a criminal prosecution may be examined and used by the accused.[56]

In a democracy, many interests bombard the legislative and executive branches for special favors. Some want old laws repealed or new ones passed; some want special privileges not shared by the average citizen, as for example the creation of exemptions in tax laws. These groups are lobbyists and must register under a federal law, disclosing who their principals are. Most special groups have such people representing them in the nation's capital. Moreover, the Congressmen that make up the House of Representatives and the Senators (two from each State) represent the special interests of their own areas; and those interests differ from State to State. The President, however, is chosen by all the people. He represents no special area, no special segment of the populace. As President Truman said: "It is only the President who is responsible to all the people. He alone has no sectional, no occupational, no economic ties.

If anyone is to speak for the people, it has to be the President." [57]

There are times when the center of power in the United States seems to be in Congress. But it is in the White House and the office of the President. Some Presidents have used little of it. Others, like Lincoln and Franklin D. Roosevelt, fully exploited it to lift the sights of the people, to summon them to difficult tasks, to change the course of history. In 1962 Kennedy used the fullness of his powers to make the steel industry rescind its price increase. Some of the powers he used were in the arsenal of law enforcement, such as the authority to enforce anti-trust laws. He also used indignation to arouse public opinion. Critics called his actions "coercive." Evil Presidents might indeed use laws as blackmail to force the opposition into line. This has not appeared on the American scene. The powers of the President, though awesome, have customarily been tempered by goodwill. Goodwill and a tolerance for the opposition, as well as for the other branches of the government, have usually been reflected in every exercise of the Presidential power.

The Legislative Power

The legislative power is the lawmaking authority; it is the branch of government that levies taxes and raises revenue; it has broad powers of investigation. Moreover, Congress has increasingly provided for the participation of its committees in executive action. Beginning in 1944 Congress provided [58] that the Navy—an executive arm—should not undertake certain construction without getting the approval of designated Congressional Committees of the details of the project. Truman in 1951 vetoed another bill of that character, saying it violated the doctrine of separation of powers. Wilson and Hoover vetoed bills containing similar provisions.[59] Eisenhower in 1954 vetoed a like measure. Yet today a military construction statute [60] contains a similar provision.

Between 1949 and 1962 the issue as to the extent of the Presidential prerogative as Commander-in-Chief was raised over and over again by the Committee on Armed Services of the House of Representatives. Article 1, Section 8 of the Constitution grants Congress the following powers:

> To raise and support Armies, but no Appropriation of Money to that Use shall be for a longer Term than two Years;
> To provide and maintain a Navy;
> To make Rules for the Government and Regulation of the land and naval forces.

The Committee maintained that Congress by appropriating money for specific purposes had the authority to require the President to spend the money for those purposes. The Presidents, Truman, Eisenhower, and Kennedy, each refused to be bound by the decision of Congress and instead of spending the appropriation for the items or projects enumerated by Congress impounded the money. The House Committee in 1962 reviewed the situation, saying:

> . . . might we not liken the function of the President to that of a general who has complete command over his forces but who can not dictate the precise weapons with which his forces will be armed. The decision as to the kind of rifle, the type of tank, and the configuration of the airplane has already been decided by other authority and the material furnished him for his use.
> Does the enactment of laws by the Congress which

provide direction to the course of our defense restrict
it to the passive role of supine acquiescence in programs
handed to it by the Department of Defense? [61]

These statements reflect a struggle for power by the
legislative branch at the expense of the executive. It is of
course the duty of the President to "execute the laws" that
Congress enacts. But the manner in which he chooses to
do so is a Presidential prerogative. And the President as
Commander-in-Chief will not be told by Congress "the
kind of rifle, the type of tank, and the configuration of the
airplane" to use.

While the President may veto an Act of Congress by
returning it to the Congress "with his objections," a veto
may be overridden by a two-thirds vote of Congress. That
is a legislative power that is occasionally exercised. If the
President does not return a bill within ten days, it becomes
a law. There is a provision in the Constitution, however,
that prevents the veto power from being defeated by a
sudden adjournment of Congress before the President has
had time to consider the bills passed. If Congress adjourns
before the ten days are up, an unsigned bill does not become a law.[62] That veto is called the "pocket veto"—the
figure of speech that depicts the President putting the bill
in his pocket and so defeating it.

While Congress is the lawmaking authority, the Constitution places restraints on it which the judicial branch
applies. The examples are numerous. Thus the courts have
held laws to be in violation of Due Process when they are
so vague that they provide no ascertainable standard of
guilt. In one such instance, a law made criminal the making of "any unjust or unreasonable rate or charge in han-
dling or dealing in or with" food supplies that were neces-

sary to life. The standard was held to be too vague to warn men when they were in violation of it.[63]

In another case, a criminal prosecution was brought for refusal to allow an inspection of a factory under the Food, Drug, and Cosmetic Act. The Act allowed inspection after officers first made a request and obtained permission. One owner withheld permission; and the Court was asked to read the law as making criminal his refusal to allow inspection at any reasonable time. The Court would not do so, saying it was "not fair warning . . . to the factory manager that if he fails to give consent, he is a criminal. The vice of vagueness in criminal statutes is the treachery they conceal either in determining what persons are included or what acts are prohibited. Words which are vague and fluid . . . may be as much of a trap for the innocent as the ancient laws of Caligula." [64] He was the Roman Emperor who "published the law, but it was written in a very small hand, and posted up to a corner, so that no one could make a copy of it." [65]

All the powers of our federal government must be exercised by one of the three departments and not delegated to private groups. In the *Schechter* case [66] the power to provide in a code the hours of work, wages, etc., in the poultry industry had been delegated by Congress to members of this industry. The Court held, in a prosecution for violation of the code, that only Congress could make a code; that Congress could not delegate to a private group —or even to the President—the power to make laws.

There are many powers which may be assigned to one or the other of the two departments, or delegated to a commission created for the purpose of administering a law or a regulation. Railroads, trucks, and buses are regulated this way. So are radio and television and the interstate transmission of gas and electricity. Labor relations are regulated. Drugs and food are inspected in the interest of health. Commissions, bureaus, and officers exercise both administrative and quasi-judicial functions.

Congress may not only create these instrumentalities, but it may delegate to them the power of making subordinate rules and the additional power of determining facts to which the policy of Congress shall apply. Such regulations, however, are valid only when subordinate to a legislative policy sufficiently defined by statute and when found to be within the framework of such policy. A delegation of legislative power to an administrative officer is not valid unless the standard for the officer's actions is fixed by Congress. Officers and agencies are not authorized to act by whim or caprice.

One important power of Congress is the power to investigate. There is no provision in the Constitution which in stated terms gives Congress that authority. Like the authority of the President to withhold from the public and from the press information in the executive branch when disclosure would be inimical to the public interest, the power of Congress to make investigations is implied. It is a necessary power—one of the most important in the congressional arsenal. Without it, Congress might not be able to know how the laws it had made were operating. Without it, Congress might not be able to learn whether the conditions in certain areas made new legislation desirable or imperative.

The first investigation by Congress was in 1792. A committee looked into the reasons why General St. Clair was defeated by American Indians. Since 1925 we have had over 500 congressional investigations in America. Many state legislatures have also made investigations.

Congress has the power to subpoena witnesses to appear and to produce papers. If the witness refuses, Congress can hold him in contempt and imprison him without resort to the courts. But Congress can imprison a recalcitrant witness only during the session of the particular Congress.[67]

A statute provides, however, that a recalcitrant witness can be prosecuted for contempt of Congress. The procedure is for Congress to pass a resolution citing the man for contempt. The case is then referred to the prosecutor; and if an indictment is returned, the person is tried by the courts. But once he is so tried, all the protective procedures of the Bill of Rights come into play—the right to jury trial, the right to counsel, etc.

The courts will not convict a witness if the question asked by the committee is beyond the competency of the committee. If a committee is authorized to investigate an air accident, it would not be permitted to ask questions concerning labor unions or price fixing.

A committee cannot investigate a judge, except through the impeachment process.

A committee cannot investigate a man's religion because Congress cannot legislate respecting religion.

A committee cannot investigate a man for making a speech because Congress has no power to legislate concerning speech.

A legislature cannot investigate an editor for his editorial because Congress cannot legislate concerning the press.

Suppose a man appeals to the people or to the Congress to discontinue a congressional investigation. Can he be investigated? Certainly not; because the First Amendment gives every man the right to petition his government, and Congress cannot legislate on that matter. As the Court held in 1955, the power of Congress to investigate "cannot be used to inquire into private affairs unrelated to a valid legislative purpose." [68]

Congressional investigations are limited in still another way. The Fifth Amendment provides that no person shall be compelled in any criminal case to be a witness against himself. A congressional investigation is not a criminal case; but the evidence given in a congressional investigation may be used in a criminal prosecution. Hence the privilege may be asserted in the investigation.[69] To compel a witness to testify over his objection based on self-incrimination, Congress must give complete immunity to the witness.[70] We now have the Compulsory Testimony Act which enables the witness to testify freely and yet be protected from prosecution for what he reveals.

The restraints on the legislative branch, like those on the executive, were addressed to specific abuses that American, British, and European experience had disclosed. The restraints on the legislative department are more numerous than those on the executive because of the broad sweep of powers granted the Congress by the federal Constitution and state legislatures by state constitutions. The fear of legislatures is embedded in Western political thought. Bagehot wrote: "A legislative chamber is greedy and covetous; it acquires as much, it concedes as little as possible. The passions of its members are its rulers; the law-making faculty, the most comprehensive of the imperial faculties, is its instrument; it will *take* the administration if it can take it." [71]

Jefferson in a letter to Madison, March 15, 1789, said: "The tyranny of the legislature is really the danger most to be feared, and will continue to be so for many years to come." [72]

A majority of the people can act as tyrannically as a king or a dictator. Madison spoke of the dangers of "factious majorities." [73]

De Tocqueville stated the matter succinctly: "A majority taken collectively is only an individual, whose opinions, and frequently whose interests, are opposed to those of another individual, who is styled a minority. If it be admitted that a man possessing absolute power may misuse that power by wronging his adversaries, why should not a majority be liable to the same approach? Men do not change their characters by uniting with one another; nor does their patience in the presence of obstacles increase with their strength." [74]

This fear of the legislature led to a long chapter in American history when its powers were drastically restricted. The Fourteenth Amendment bars a state (as the Fifth Amendment bars Congress) from depriving any person "of life, liberty, or property without due process of law." "Liberty" was held to include "liberty of contract"; and in 1905, the Supreme Court held that regulation of working hours was an interference with that "liberty." [75] Laws fixing minimum wages later met the same fate.[76] So did a law outlawing discharge of employees for their union activities.[77] The examples are almost legion. They cover the span of years from the 1880s into the 1930s.

But the tide turned and the legislative powers were restored. A Missouri law gave employees time off to vote and made it unlawful for an employer to deduct wages for their absence. The Court said: "The public welfare is a broad and inclusive concept. The moral, social, economic, and physical well-being of the community is one part of it; the political well-being, another. The police power which is adequate to fix the financial burden for one is adequate for the other. The judgment of the legislature that time out for voting should cost the employee nothing may be a debatable one. It is indeed conceded by the opposition to be such. But if our recent cases mean anything, they leave debatable issues as respects business, economic, and social affairs to legislative decision." [78]

The sweep of the police power of the legislature under modern decisions is shown by a case involving the condemnation of property in slum areas for a redevelopment project. The Court said:

> Public safety, public health, morality, peace and quiet, law and order—these are some of the more conspicuous examples of the traditional application of the police power to municipal affairs. Yet they merely illustrate the scope of the power and do not delimit it. . . . Miserable and disreputable housing conditions may do more than spread disease and crime and immorality. They may also suffocate the spirit by reducing the people who live there to the status of cattle. They may indeed make living an almost insufferable burden. They may also be an ugly sore, a blight on the community which robs it of charm, which makes it a place from which men turn. The misery of housing may despoil a community as an open sewer may ruin a river.
>
> We do not sit to determine whether a particular housing project is or is not desirable. The concept of the public welfare is broad and inclusive. . . . The values it represents are spiritual as well as physical, aesthetic as well as monetary. It is within the power of the legislature to determine that the community should be beautiful as well as healthy, spacious as well as clean, well-balanced as well as carefully patrolled. In the present case, the Congress and its authorized agencies have made determinations that take into account a wide variety of values.

It is not for us to reappraise them. If those who govern the District of Columbia decide that the Nation's Capital should be beautiful as well as sanitary, there is nothing in the Fifth Amendment that stands in the way.[79]

Man's liberty is, of course, often related to his property rights. The home and its privacy are property interests. Ownership of a press is essential to the freedom granted newspapers, magazines, pamphlets, and books. Ownership of a cathedral or church is basic to the free exercise of religion by those whose faith brings them together into congregations. These cannot be taken away without impairing the right. No property may be taken "for a public purpose" either by a State or by the federal government without "just compensation." And that property right extends to the use of the air over a person's land so as to impair its use either for an agricultural purpose [80] or as a residence.[81] Flights of airplanes at low altitudes may in other words constitute a taking of an air easement for which the government must pay.

In no part of American law is confiscation of property permitted. A State, if it chooses, may adopt a socialist economy.[82] But to do so it must pay for the private property which it converts to public use. By "just compensation" is meant "the full and perfect equivalent in money of the property taken," [83] which usually is what a willing buyer would pay in cash to a willing seller.

The powers of Congress are commonly spoken of as being "legislative"; and so they are, in the main. But some of the powers of Congress have a judicial flavor. Thus each House is given by the Constitution the power to judge the elections, returns, and qualifications of its members. Incidental to that power is the power to ascertain the facts concerning the elections in order to discover whether there was fraud or any irregularity. Thus either the Senate or the House may inquire into the elections, summon witnesses, reject the credentials of one candidate, and accept those of another. "In exercising the power to judge of the elections, returns and qualifications of its members, the Senate acts as a judicial tribunal, and the authority to require the attendance of witnesses is a necessary incident of the power to adjudge, in no wise inferior under like circumstances to that exercised by a court of justice." [84] Neither the judiciary nor the executive can interfere with the Senate or the House in its determination as to which of several contenders for a seat should be recognized as the lawful claimant.

The Judicial Power

An independent judiciary is a *sine qua non* of a Free Society. Where judges are subservient to the executive or legislative power, they become instruments for expressing the whim or caprice of those in power. Our Declaration of Independence from England complained that the King "has made judges dependent on his will alone, for the tenure of their offices, and the amount and payment of their salaries."

James Wilson, one of the authors of the Constitution, spoke of the evils of a union of legislative and judicial powers: ". . . The lives, liberties, and properties of the citizens would be committed to arbitrary judges, whose decisions would, in effect, be dictated by their own private opinions, and would not be governed by any fixed or known principles of law. For though, as judges, they might be bound to observe those principles; yet, Proteus-like, they might immediately assume the form of legislators; and, in

that shape, they might escape from every fetter and obligation of law."

He also spoke of the evils of the executive and judicial
power being united: ". . . Nothing is more to be dreaded
than maxims of law and reasons of state blended together
by judicial authority. Among all the terrible instruments of
arbitrary power, decisions of courts, whetted and guided
and impelled by considerations of policy, cut with the
keenest edge, and inflict the deepest and most deadly
wounds." [85] Trujillo subverted the constitution of the Do-
minican Republic by obtaining from every judge he swore
in an undated letter of resignation, Trujillo filling in the
date when he became displeased with the judge's decisions.

The need in any society is for an arbiter who is not
swayed by the passions of the day but who dispenses equal
justice to minorities and majorities alike.

In some of the American states the judges of the state
courts are appointed by the Governor for a fixed term.
About three-fourths of our states elect most or all of their
judges. In the federal system, the judges are nominated by
the President and confirmed by the Senate, as provided
by the Constitution. They hold their offices "during good
behavior," which means they serve for life unless they re-
sign, or unless they retire at full salary (as they may do at
the age of 65 provided they have served fifteen years, or at
the age of 70 provided they have served ten years). They
may be impeached, as provided in the Constitution, by the
House of Representatives. If a judge is impeached, the
Senate sits as a court to determine guilt or innocence, the
vote of two-thirds of the members of the Senate present
being necessary for conviction.

The independence of the judiciary is protected by mak-

ing removal of judges difficult, because "a fear of dis-
pleasing the legislature may always hover over the mind of
the judge, and prevent his being the impartial and in-
flexible mediator between the legislature and the people,
which the people intended he should be." [86]

The impeachment power over federal judges has been
sparingly used. The Senate has sat in only nine cases involving judicial officers. Of these, one resigned, four were
acquitted, and four were removed from office. Of the nine,
only one was a member of the Supreme Court. He was
Justice Samuel Chase, and the independence of the federal judiciary from political manipulation was clearly established by his acquittal in 1805.

Chase had given intemperate rulings in cases under the
Alien and Sedition Acts, and the political hounds in pursuit used impeachment as their weapon. Those Acts had
become an intense political issue between Jefferson, who
was a Republican, and Adams, who was a Federalist. All
five members of the Court were Federalist appointees. In
1803 they had incurred the wrath of the Republicans in
declaring that the Court had the power to declare Acts of
Congress unconstitutional.[87]

The articles of impeachment against Chase, who had
been appointed by Washington, read today more like
a lawyer's appeal in a criminal case than "misbehavior" in
the constitutional sense. The Senate acquitted Chase; and
the trial record is replete with Americana. One of Chase's
lawyers, Robert G. Harper, said to the Senate sitting as a
court in the Chase trial:

> Let them remember, that power must often change
> hands in popular governments; and that after every
> struggle, the victorious party comes into power, with

resentments to gratify by the destruction of their van-
quished opponents, with a thirst of vengeance to be
slaked in their blood. Let them remember, that principles
and precedents, by which actions innocent when they
were done may be converted into crimes, are the most
convenient and effectual instruments of revenge and destruction, with which a victorious party can be furnished.
Let them beware how they give their sanction to principles, which may soon be turned against themselves;
how they forge bolts which may soon be hurled on their
own heads. In a popular government, where power is so
fluctuating, where constitutional principles are therefore
so important for the protection of the weaker party
against the violence of the stronger, it above all things
behooves the party actually in power, to adhere to the
principles of justice and law; lest by departing from them
they furnish at once the provocation and the weapons,
for their own destruction.[88]

In 1953, when a House Committee, investigating grand
jury proceedings, subpoenaed the late Louis Goodman, a
federal District Judge, he replied:

. . . The judges signing below, being all the judges of
the court, are deeply conscious, as must be your committee, of the constitutional separation of functions
among the executive, legislative, and judicial branches of
the Federal Government. This separation of functions is
founded on the historic concept that no one of these
branches may dominate or unlawfully interfere with the
others.

In recognition of the fundamental soundness of this
principle we are unwilling that a judge of this court appear before your committee and testify with respect to
any judicial proceeding. The Constitution of the United

States does not contemplate that such matters be reviewed by the legislative branch, but only by the appropriate appellate tribunals. The integrity of the Federal
courts, upon which liberty and life depend, requires that
such courts be maintained inviolate against the changing
moods of public opinion. We are certain that you as legislators have always appreciated and recognized this, and
we know of no instance in the history of the United
States where a committee such as yours has summoned
a member of the Federal judiciary. . . .[89]

Since one way of controlling judges is reducing their
salaries once their decisions become unpopular with those
in power, the Constitution provides that federal judges
shall "receive for their Services a Compensation which
shall not be diminished during their continuance in Office." [90] In 1920 the Court held that this provision rendered unconstitutional the taxation of income of federal
judges as part of a taxing measure of general non-discriminatory application.[91] Later, Congress provided that United
States judges appointed after the Revenue Act of 1932
should not enjoy immunity from taxation. Once more the
Court was confronted with the problem. The Court, in
dealing with the case of a judge who had been appointed
to his office after 1932 and had thus been forewarned of
the Congressional intent to tax his income, upheld the
validity of the tax: "To suggest that it makes inroads upon
the independence of judges who took office after Congress
had thus charged them with the common duties of citizenship, by making them bear their aliquot share of the cost
of maintaining the Government, is to trivialize the great
historic experience on which the framers based the safeguards of the Constitution." [92]

When the Supreme Court in 1803 announced it would

review the constitutionality of federal laws, Chief Justice Marshall said:

> It is emphatically the province and duty of the judicial department to say what the law is. Those who apply the rule to particular cases, must of necessity expound and interpret that rule. If two laws conflict with each other, the courts must decide on the operation of each.
>
> So if a law be in opposition to the constitution; if both the law and the constitution apply to a particular case, so that the court must either decide that case conformably to the law, disregarding the constitution; or conformably to the constitution, disregarding the law; the court must determine which of these conflicting rules governs the case. This is of the very essence of judicial duty.[93]

This power of declaring unconstitutional the action of the President or laws passed by Congress is sparingly used. If a construction of the Act is possible that will save it from being constitutionally infirm, the Court will adopt that construction.[94]

The theory behind this curb on legislative and executive action was explained by James Madison: "In the United States . . . The People, not the Government, possess the absolute sovereignty. The Legislature, no less than the Executive, is under limitations of power. Encroachments are regarded as possible from the one as well as from the other. Hence, in the United States the great and essential rights of the people are secured against legislative as well as against executive ambition. They are secured, not by laws paramount to prerogative, but by constitutions paramount to laws." [95]

The United States has a dual system of courts—a fed-

eral judiciary operating cooperatively with a system of
state courts. The federal system derives from Article III,
Section 1 of the Constitution, which vests "the judicial
Power" of the United States "in one Supreme Court, and
in such inferior Courts as the Congress may from time to
time ordain and establish." This is the provision that authorizes Congress to create the federal system of courts.
It is this dual system that has given rise to delicate and
perplexing problems of federalism.

The judicial power of the state courts is defined by the
constitutions and laws of the several States. Since the state
courts are creatures of the respective States, they can have
such power as their own constitutions and laws provide, as
long as that power does not conflict with the federal Constitution. Some ten of the States authorize their courts to
render advisory opinions.[96]

Whether these advisory opinions serve an important
function is a debatable issue. Sometimes legislators refer
proposed legislation to the courts for advisory opinions,
either for delay or in the hope that the judges will declare
the bill unconstitutional and thus save the legislators from
going on record either for or against the measure. Whatever may be said of the advisory opinion, it is an established institution in a number of States.

The Constitution of the United States does not permit
federal courts to render advisory opinions. Article III,
Section 2 extends the judicial power only to "cases" or
"controversies." This power embraces only actual disputes
between persons or between a person and the government.
In 1793, President Washington caused a letter to be sent by
Jefferson, Secretary of State, to the Supreme Court asking
whether the President might seek their advice on questions
of law arising out of treaties which the United States had

entered into with certain foreign nations. The Court refused to entertain the question, pointing out that while the Constitution expressly grants the President power to call on the heads of departments for opinions, it contains no such provision as respects the judiciary. The Court wrote in reply that the three departments of government being "in certain respects checks upon each other and our being Judges of a Court in the last resort," were "considerations which afford strong arguments against the propriety of our extra-judicially deciding the questions alluded to." This decision led the historian Charles Warren to say, "By the firm stand thus taken at so early a stage in the career of the new Government, and by declining to express an opinion except in a case duly litigated before it, the Court established itself as a purely judicial body." [97]

Congress determines the time when court terms begin and end; it determines what the quorum necessary for the making of a decision is; it determines the number of judges that make up the Supreme Court and the lower federal courts; it makes the appropriations necessary for doing the judicial work. But it does not and cannot define with finality what is the meaning of "judicial power" within the meaning of the Constitution. For that is a problem of construction for the judiciary.

It is essential first that the duties assigned the courts be compatible with the judicial function. Judicial power does not exist where a branch of the executive department or the Congress can accept or reject the decision or, if it calls for the payment of money, can reduce the amount awarded.[98]

The requirement of the Constitution that judicial power be exerted only over "cases" or "controversies" not only precludes the rendering of advisory opinions, but also prohibits judicial decision in any case where the litigation, though in form a "controversy," is in fact only a friendly lawsuit designed to get a ruling from the federal courts. The courts may not reach a decision where the litigation in the courts is premature, there being administrative remedies that need first to be exhausted; nor where the particular plaintiff has no standing to sue or where his interest is nebulous and remote.

While there is no quarrel over these principles, their application has led to inconsistent decisions; the trend has been to close the doors of the federal courts to many vivid controversies. Examples are the refusal to allow taxpayers standing to challenge the constitutionality of a federal law [99] or a state law.[100] Moreover, a physician and his patients were not allowed standing to challenge state birth control laws, absent a criminal prosecution against them.[101] A government employee, barred by Civil Service rules from engaging in political activities, had no standing to challenge those restrictions where he had not risked his job by indulging in the prohibited activities.[102] The list is long and the decisions are not easily reconciled.

There are two decisions that reflect the solicitude of the judiciary for solution of controversies which, though involving no clash with the police, involve conditions that put the citizen into a position of peril and insecurity. The first involved a suit by a Negro who purchased a first-class railroad ticket but was refused admission to first-class coaches and was compelled to ride in a second-class car. His standing to seek relief before the Interstate Commerce Commission and the federal courts was challenged. The Court said: "Nor is it determinative that it does not appear that appellant intends to make a similar railroad journey. He is an American citizen free to travel, and he is entitled to go by this particular route whenever he chooses to take it and in that event to have facilities for his journey without any discrimination against him which the Interstate Commerce Act forbids. He presents the question whether the Act does forbid the conduct of which he complains." [103]

In the second case a Negro was allowed standing to challenge the segregation of races on municipal buses though he had ridden a segregated bus only once and even then was not arrested for sitting in the "white" section. The Court said: "We do not believe that appellant, in order to demonstrate the existence of an 'actual controversy' over the validity of the statute here challenged, was bound to continue to ride the Memphis buses at the risk of arrest if he refused to seat himself in the space in such vehicles assigned to colored passengers. A resident of a municipality who cannot use transportation facilities therein without being subjected by statute to special disabilities necessarily has, we think, a substantial, immediate, and real interest in the validity of the statute which imposes the disability." [104]

A real controversy may of course become moot. The party against whom an order was sought to be enforced may die; the law on which the complaint rests may be repealed; or other conduct or intervening events may for all practical purposes bring the controversy to an end. The practice in such cases is to reverse or vacate the judgment below and remand the cause with directions to dismiss the complaint on the grounds of mootness.[105] That order eliminates from the books a decision rendered on facts presenting no justiciable question and yet which in the future might be invoked as a precedent.

This does not mean that the voluntary cessation of the challenged conduct deprives the judicial body of the power to determine the case.[106] If it did, the wrongdoer could

easily escape by using the doctrine of "case" or "controversy" for dilatory tactics. As long as there is an actual
or threatened invasion of a private or public right, the
judicial power to deal with it survives intervening events
that do not bring the controversy to a practical end.

Normally, service of a sentence will render the case
moot, since there will no longer be a subject matter on
which the judgment of the Court can operate.[107] But a
judgment of conviction may have consequences that survive the service of a sentence. Convicted felons often lose
civil rights by the law of the state of their residence, e.g.,
the right to serve on a jury, the right to vote, the right to
hold office. If the convicted felon is an alien, the judgment
may be the basis of his deportation; or it may stand as a
barrier to his naturalization. If further penalties or disabilities can be imposed the legal consequences of the
judgment of conviction have not been wholly dissipated.
In that event, the defendant may have his case reviewed on
the merits and it will not be dismissed as moot, even though
he has served the sentence pending appeal.[108]

Not until 1855 did Congress authorize certain suits
against the United States. Not until 1946, when the Tort
Claims Act was enacted, was it possible for a citizen to sue
the United States for torts committed by government serv-
ants. In early English history the King's will was law. He
appointed the judges who spoke in his stead and on his
behalf. He was their source of authority. They sat at his
will and often were instruments of his political designs.
The courts, being his instruments, would entertain no suits
or complaints against him. He was immune from all suits
because judges subservient to his will obviously could not
entertain them. This doctrine of sovereign immunity became detached from its origins and was adopted by the

American courts, though the reason for its creation no longer was relevant once America won her independence from England.

The relation of the King to British courts has had a continuing influence with us. In 1460 the House of Lords was presented with the claim of the Duke of York to have himself declared the rightful heir to the throne. The Lords, as ordered by the King, asked the King's Justices to assist them. The judges refused to rule, saying they "durst not enter into eny communication thereof, for it perteyned to the Lordes of the Kyngs blode." [109] By 1793, the principle that courts will not interfere with "political" questions was firmly established in English law. When the Nabob sued the East India Company for breach of contract, the English courts refused to entertain the action, saying that the East India Company, in making contracts with foreign potentates, was acting as delegate of the Crown and for its action could not be held accountable in the courts of law.[110]

That kind of question is known in America as a "case" or "controversy" that involves a "political" question which the courts will not resolve.

One group involves the duty of a governor of a State to deliver up fugitives to the authorities of another State under the customary extradition procedure. While the Constitution says that the fugitive "shall . . . be delivered up," the Court says that it is the sense of the Constitution to leave the "performance of this duty" to "the fidelity of the State Executive." [111]

The examples are numerous where an officer is entrusted with duties which are entirely discretionary. No court could compel the exercise of the discretion one way or the other without taking over the office.

Another group of cases involving the so-called "political

question" concerns functions assigned by the Constitution exclusively to particular departments. Thus, when the Court must determine whether or not a particular treaty has survived a war between two nations, the Court will not make this decision independently, but will, as already noted, first determine what the policy of the executive and legislative departments has been as respects the survival of a particular treaty. It does this on the theory that the treaty-making power is committed by the Constitution to the President and Senate.[112]

The power to conduct foreign affairs includes, of course, the power to recognize a particular regime as the *de jure* or *de facto* sovereign of another nation. When the political branches of government have spoken, the judiciary is bound. The propriety of such political action is not open to judicial inquiry or decision.[113] Whether dominion over new territory has been acquired by discovery and occupation, by cession or by conquest, the judiciary may not question it.[114]

There is a difference, however, between questioning the actual exercise of power specifically given to one department, and reviewing justiciable issues which may arise from its action. Thus, private rights may flow from a treaty.[115] Similarly, although the President as Commander-in-Chief makes decisions in which no one else can participate, his actions may give rise to claims that courts will adjudicate.[116] This was the blind spot of the Court in deciding a case involving the grant of certificates for overseas airlines service. Since the grant was subject to the President's approval, the Court decided that the matter was "political" and refused to adjudicate the issues involved.[117]

The problem of legislative reapportionment, always troublesome, has until recently been regarded as "political" by some courts. Each State historically has determined how many electoral districts there shall be and how many representatives shall be chosen from each district to serve in the state legislature. Sometimes a State has given a thinly settled agricultural district as many representatives as a populous urban district. Thus a farmer's vote may have ten or twenty times the strength of a city person's vote. Legislatures dominated, say, by the rural vote have sometimes refused to reapportion the State so as more nearly to equalize the votes of the rural people and the city people.

As stated by the Supreme Court of New Jersey: "If by reason of passage of time and changing conditions the re-apportionment statute no longer serves its original purpose of securing to the voter the full constitutional value of his franchise, and the legislative branch fails to take appropriate restorative action, the doors of the courts must be open to him. The law-making body cannot by inaction alter the constitutional system under which it has its own existence." [118]

That view, once rejected by the federal Supreme Court, was at long last accepted by it in 1962.[119] The judiciary does not make the reapportionment. It issues its mandate to the appropriate state officials to draw the electoral lines so that no segment of the population suffers an invidious discrimination.

The Court also struck down a state law which reduced the vote of Negroes, Catholics, or Jews so that each got only one-tenth of a vote. It recently held that a city could not redraw its city limits so as to exclude Negroes from voting in municipal elections, since the Fifteenth Amendment forbids a State from passing any law that deprives a person of his vote by reason of his race.[120]

The judiciary plainly has a restricted role. It does not

fashion policies. It may be impractical for a court to undertake to formulate a decree in some cases. Yet once a "case" or "controversy" arises, it should be subject to adjudication in the court unless the subject matter has been wholly and indivisibly entrusted by the Constitution to another branch. The "political" question has been too frequently used as a thicket behind which the judiciary retreats. It is becoming more and more apparent, as affairs become more and more complicated, that absent a judicial remedy for a wrong there may be none within the reach of the average person.

A strong independent judiciary is a bulwark of the people. If the judiciary bows to expediency and puts questions in the "political" rather than in the justiciable category merely because they are troublesome or embarrassing or pregnant with great emotion, the judiciary has become a political instrument itself. Courts sit to determine questions on stormy as well as on calm days. The Constitution is the measure of their duty. And it is the Constitution, not the judges' individual preferences, that marks the line between what is justiciable on the one hand and, on the other, what is political and therefore beyond the reach or competence of courts.

Man's long struggle has been to live under a government of laws, not of men. Man's search has been for equal justice under law, for a system of law applicable to all alike. Man has sought to escape the regime that dispenses justice according to the political or religious ideology of the litigant or the whim or caprice of the government official.

A judiciary dedicated to a government of laws creates confidence in the body politic and a sense of responsibility both in lawmakers and in those who administer the law.

The present President of India in an address before the

American Congress summed up one important aspect of
both the Indian and American philosophy of government:
"The end of all governments is to give a status of social
equality and provide economic opportunity for the common people. We, in our country, are now engaged in the
enterprise of effecting a social and economic revolution.
The word 'revolution' need not scare us. It does not mean
barricades and bloodshed. It means only speedy and
drastic changes. We are interested not only in our objectives, but in our methods; not only in what we achieve,
but in how we achieve." [121]

We reject the philosophy that the end justifies the means.
The vitality of human rights means respect for procedure
as well as respect for substantive rights. A court cannot
render dispassionate justice in the presence of a howling
mob. History shows that man's struggle to be free is in a
large degree the struggle to be free of oppressive procedures.

That is the real significance of the separation of powers
and the checks and balances in the American system.

We do not entrust all power to any group. Even the
judiciary is subject to procedural restraints.

The secret trial is not constitutional. The trial must be
"public." Long detention is not permitted. The trial must
be "speedy." The accused must be tried where the crime
was committed, not whisked away to a community where
he has no friends. Confessions coerced from an accused
may not be used in evidence. Police may not enter homes
and offices at will; they need a search warrant issued by a
judge on a showing of probable cause. If they proceed
lawlessly, the evidence they acquire is not admissible
against the accused. The judge may not impose "cruel and
unusual" punishment. An accused is normally entitled to

bail; and it shall not be made "excessive" by the judge. If an accused does not have a lawyer to defend him, the judge must assign one. And most important of all—in all criminal cases (and in civil cases at law where the amount in controversy is twenty dollars or more), there must be a jury trial, unless of course it is waived. This is an important guarantee because history shows that judges—as well as kings and legislatures—have at times been tyrants. A man is more apt to get justice if he is judged by his peers, not by a judge who may be calloused or prejudiced.

Judges, though independent of the executive and the legislative, have also been placed in harness. The Constitution protects the people against their excesses as well as the ambitions of the executive and the passions of the legislative.

There are many areas where the lines of authority between the three branches of the American government are indistinct. It will probably never be possible to mark all the limits with precision. It would be a needless undertaking. Where there are clashes and conflicts, they are resolved by amicable settlements. Goodwill is the most important solvent of problems. The courts indulge in presumptions that no law violates the Constitution; and they avoid adjudications on constitutional issues if a controversy can be resolved on other grounds. The Chief Executive and the Congress, though frequently disagreeing with the courts, respect their function. A sober second look at legislation and a redrafting to meet constitutional objections involve delay. But that is one price paid for any system of checks and balances. It has not proved costly, though it has at times set back some political programs. The life of the nation surges forward; and all the while the tradition of the Rule of Law becomes more and more the pattern.

Political differences continue; yet personal dislikes do not disrupt the system or lead to vindictive action. The *consensus* for the division of powers grows. The cementing influence of goodwill makes the American experiment enduring. Without that goodwill, what is written on parchment would be transitory, not enduring.

THE UNITED NATIONS
AND A RULE OF LAW

> *"The structure of world peace cannot be the work of one man, or one party, or one nation. It cannot be just an American peace, or a British peace, or a Russian, a French or a Chinese peace. It cannot be a peace of large nations—or of small nations. It must be a peace which rests on the cooperative effort of the whole world."*
> —FRANKLIN D. ROOSEVELT

> *"There can be no peace for any part of the world unless the foundations of peace are made secure throughout all parts of the world."*
> —WENDELL WILLKIE

MAN'S SECURITY was once the family, then the tribe, and finally the nation. Now his security lies in supranational arrangements over which he has little control. These arrangements involve people of whom he is ignorant and foreign leaders he has never met. Those who formed communities or nations moved to the impulse of common needs or common ambitions. They found unity in the common defense, in the common market, or in a unity of religious faith. Now the sheer necessity to avoid the nuclear holocaust makes it necessary for us to build unity in common goals of an international character.

The problem of survival turns on finding ways and means to maintain a Rule of Law in world affairs that takes the place of force—now obsolete.

The Rule of Law is the only solution to the world's problems in this nuclear age. The physicists have told us how obsolete the cult of force, armed with nuclear weapons, has become. Harrison Brown and James Real show in their book how and why America could today probably be utterly destroyed by less than a 20,000-megaton attack.[1]

Hans Bethe, Cornell's nuclear and theoretical physicist, recently stated: "The scientist looked into the hell of the bomb long before anybody else did. One of the things that troubles me is that nobody believes us when we predict the hell, and that even the responses we scientists make to the hell, both inside and outside government, are not appropriate to the magnitude of that hell." [2]

The tendency has been to shut our eyes to the awful consequences of atomic war. We do not like to think in human terms of what was done to the people of Hiroshima. As Clyde Eatherly, the conscience-stricken navigator on that fateful flight, wrote in 1959: "The truth is that society simply cannot accept the fact of my guilt without at the same time recognizing its own far deeper guilt." [3]

Today there are only a few nations that have nuclear weapons. In ten to twenty years how many nations will not have the secret? We are told that at least fifteen nations will be producing nuclear weapons in the 1960s, including Peking.

When atomic bombs, as a result of new discoveries, get

into "the ten dollar" class, what international gangster will be without one? What Hitler will appear with mad dreams? What leader with cold calculation may be willing to sacrifice twenty million, a hundred million, or even more of his own people to conquer the world through a sudden nuclear attack?

The greater risks may indeed lie in conflicts in the minor nuclear club, rather than in the major one. What small nation may not see the end of her pestiferous neighbor by dropping only one nuclear bomb? What chain reaction may that produce?

People the world over are disturbed by these thoughts. Reason, as well as fear, is propelling them to place their hopes in joint action to protect the very earth from being so poisoned by radio-active fall-out that human life is jeopardized or even ended. Fall-out from test explosions is a major concern of public-health officials, scientists, and laymen the world around. Milk, vegetables, and fish become suspect. Trans-Atlantic and trans-Pacific planes have to be washed after every trip lest contamination reach a dangerous concentration. Russia's explosion of the 50-megaton bomb in 1961 will, it is estimated, result in the birth of 200,000 defective children.

The U. S. Public Health Service estimated that by 1962, as a result of the Russian tests, children would have in their bones double the amount of strontium 90 they had in 1961.

In 1962, within a week after the United States had resumed testing in the Pacific, the content of radio-active iodine in milk in some areas in the United States had leaped to six times the level considered acceptable by the Federal Radiation Council.

In the same year, eighteen hours after a test shot in

Nevada, a severe thunderstorm took place in Troy, New York. The radio-active fallout in Troy was measured, and discovered to have increased drastically. Dr. Ralph E. Lapp estimated that *one pint* of milk from cows feeding in Troy pastures at that time would contain *twice* the British *annual* allowance for intake of iodine-131. In Salt Lake City, following a series of Nevada tests, Utah public health authorities were actually forced to withdraw great quantities of milk from the fresh-milk market because of the enormous amounts of iodine-131 it contained. The damage this milk could do to the thyroids of milk-drinking, growing children—as well as to unborn babies and adults —is almost incomprehensible.

Contamination is so severe in upstate New York that manufacturers of sensitive articles, such as film, will not admit workers to their plants until their clothes have been changed. And some have tracking stations as far west as Hawaii to measure the volume of radio-active elements in the air and compute their arrival time in New York.

Linus Pauling, American chemist who won the Nobel Prize, claims that the resumed testing in 1961 by Russia can be compared with "the assignment of Jews to the gas chambers" by Hitler. He adds:

> The carbon 14 produced will cause an estimated total of 4 million stillbirths, embryonic, neo-natal or child-hood deaths, and viable children with physical and mental defects. These 4 million victims will be spread out over some score of generations, assuming the human race survives.
>
> We are moving rapidly toward the catastrophe of nuclear war. Survivors will not remain alive very long in the radio-active wastelands that their countries will become.[4]

The word "deterrent" falls easily from the lips of people in the United States and in Russia. It is carelessly assumed that the side that has the more effective quantity and quality of nuclear bombs can or will deter the other from using theirs. It is not proven that the prospect of terror prevents terror. We in the United States know that the death sentence is not a deterrent to murder.

While we know that armed forces are as necessary at the international level as the police and the militia are at home, history makes unmistakably clear that there is no safety or security in deterrents. Massive armaments have led to increasingly devastating wars; and war in modern terms means the extinction of civilization and perhaps of all life on all continents. Ernest Cuneo has reduced the idea to scientific terms in his new book *Science and History* (1963):

> The compulsion of nations to attempt to balance power does not balance power; on the contrary, it accelerates the acquisition of more power by each side, and has invariably resulted in war because of the reciprocal accelerating motion on the compulsions of each to match the other. Each side, in mortal fear of the other, redoubles its energies, failing to see that as it does so, it compels its adversary to do likewise. It is as impossible to freeze a balance-of-power armament race as it is to freeze two racehorses pounding down the home stretch neck and neck for the Grand Prix.
>
> The reason is that balance assumes permanent rest, permanent stabilization. This is a concept inapplicable to living things.
>
> Since the actual balance of power is conscious, it accelerates the coming of war.

Some say we could survive even if we lost 80 million

people or perhaps 100 million. Even if that were true in the technical sense, the earth and the waters would be poisoned for centuries, and man would return to the cave. Moreover, the problems that created the holocaust would survive as long as there were people on the planet. The ideas—mutually hated on both sides—would continue to compete for converts. But the devastation created by fire storms would be so great and the normal community and state activities so paralyzed that a military dictatorship would almost certainly take over—perhaps of necessity. Our Free Society would disappear; and so if one could say that our side "won," there never would have been a more disastrous or costly "victory."

Bursts of aggression appear decade after decade in recorded history. They are not peculiar to any race but common to all. We Aryans seem to have had a special capacity for aggression. When we moved down into the subcontinent of India (about 2000 B.C.) we destroyed the great civilization of Mohenjendaro on the Indus River; and the record of that destruction is recorded in the Rigveda with somewhat the same religious ecstasy as we praise the horrible deeds of our own Crusaders. We also produced Hitler. After him came Trujillo, who killed 200,000 under torture and who delighted in showing dinner guests the bodies of political enemies hanging like slabs of beef in the refrigerators of the palace.

Psychotics have often risen to positions of power; and we can safely predict they will in the future sit in the seats of the mighty. Now they have more than the catapult, more than the torture chamber, more than missiles and bombs. Now they have—or will shortly have—the nuclear bomb. Would Hitler have used it? Would he have been deterred by fear of reprisal?

Mortimer Ostrow in a recent article (Bull. Atomic Sc. Jan. 1963) says that "The impulsion to military adventure must be attributed principally to the death instinct" and that to such a person the threat of deterrent reprisal "holds no terror, in fact it invites rather than deters him." For punitive aggression, Ostrow says, "may be redirected outwards as an attack upon another individual" or directed inwardly "to eradicate" the pain of the psychotic.

Our risk of survival turns not on what "reasonable" men will do but either (1) on what a psychotic in power will do or (2) on what "reasonable" men will do when they become unreasonable under the excitement and tensions of pre-war charges and counter-charges. As Ostrow has said:

> Clearly the degree of which unconscious sadism, unconscious suicidal impulses, and unconscious hostility to his own people will influence the behavior of the leader, is neither constant from leader to leader, nor constant from time to time, nor predictable.

In quiet moments of repose most people know that there must be disarmament if civilization is to survive. Yet that issue is so clouded with emotion that it does not emerge as an increasingly imperative demand. The power of the military and the propaganda they command is one reason. The ease with which "we" can always be made to seem "righteous" and "they" made to seem "evil" is a compound of many forces. Jung said:

> The psychology of war has clearly brought this condition to light: everything which our own nation does is good, everything which the other nations do is wicked. The centre of all that is mean and vile is always to be

found several miles behind the enemy's lines. This same primitive psychology appears in the individual, so that every attempt to make these eternally unconscious projections conscious is felt to be very uncongenial. Certainly we wish to have better relations with our fellow men, but naturally on condition that our fellow men fulfil our expectations, in other words, that they are willing to carry our projections. (*Psychological Reflections* [1953], p. 136.)

Most men are able to avoid disquieting facts by employing some avenue of escape which may permit them to grasp the technical aspects of a problem but keep them distant from the psychological and political realities. Dr. Lester Grinspoon recently stated why the truth about the nature, risk, and consequences of nuclear war is unacceptable to people:

> It serves a man no useful purpose to accept this truth if to do so leads only to the development of very disquieting feelings, feelings which interfere with his capacity to be productive, to enjoy life, and to maintain his mental equilibrium.

What happens when people's means of keeping disquieting facts at bay have been suddenly broken through?

For a while, Dr. Grinspoon says, these people may suffer anxious and depressive feelings which may even be crippling. Some may even become mentally ill. Most people, however, "either reconstitute their defense mechanisms much as a self-sealing tire seals over after a puncture, or they . . . embrace some program or activity which they believe is capable of altering the unacceptable facts."

There may be other reasons why our people seem lackadaisical over the awful realities of the nuclear holocaust. Whatever all the reasons may be, we walk the brink every hour of every day.

We are driven by necessity not to imitate the military but to forsake their philosophy and look to political solutions for our salvation.

Some have the lingering notion that wars without nuclear weapons can be fought—if only nuclear weapons are abolished. That is dangerous thinking. Now that the art of making them is known, they could be quickly manufactured even though all were destroyed. They are so strategically important they would tempt any participant. Once war broke out, a frantic race would be on to manufacture again the outlawed nuclear weapons. The side that won that race would have the opponent at its mercy. We know now that nuclear war risks all life on each continent that is involved, and perhaps all other life as well. That means that the central problem of this day is the *prevention* of war. Yet the arms race continues with the nations of the world spending on armaments about $150 billion a year.

The Charter of the United Nations contains a resolve on the part of the people "to save succeeding generations from the scourge of war, which twice in our lifetime has brought untold sorrow to mankind." [5] Effective prevention of war means disarmament. Partial disarmament is a sham except insofar as it leads to the establishment of procedures which can be extended to full disarmament. The danger of partial disarmament is that each side aims to keep the weapon—or weapons—that best suit its strategic position. Pursuit of peace at this stage means making the search for fool-proof disarmament the first item on the international agenda. Walter Millis, in a challenging work, shows that a viable world could easily exist if war were actually abolished and if war never again became an instrument of national power.[6]

Full disarmament, quickly realized, is man's most difficult problem. World disarmament without including the Peking government—representing the largest block of people in the world—is only a pipe-dream. Even if all nations are included, the process is almost certain to be slow and painful. No nation has complete trust in any other nation. Each nation has its pride in sovereignty, its dreams of leadership, its tradition of independence, its reasons for suspecting the motives of others. Only a slow, gradual approach will succeed.

Inspection has so far been the actual or feigned stumbling block to any progress in disarmament. It may seem more ominous to the weaker power (Russia) than to us. Partial disarmament first, as the British physicist and Nobel Prize winner P. M. S. Blackett has suggested, followed by "international verification" [7] may be the key to the first stages. Even the sensitive problem of inspection may be solved more quickly than we now know. In time satellites may be able to photograph and report on all surface activities of a nation. International conventions for the use of satellites will—or may—control a host of international problems, including the inspection aspect of any disarmament program. The problem of disarmament is as emotional as it is military. It is not only the key to a solution of world problems. It is the key to survival. Once substantial leveling of armaments has been achieved, the design of a world without war will become clearer in the eyes of people on all continents.

Grenville Clark (long active in an endeavor to awaken our people to a need for a rule of law in world affairs) has recently described in the *Saturday Review* the need for disarmament in new dimensions. If it takes until the year of 1982 to achieve total disarmament, the world will then have about 4.4 billion of people as compared with the present population of 3.1 billion. Of these 4.4 billion, about 60 per cent, or 2.6 billion, will be living in dire poverty. Under a war economy there will be insufficient capital materially to improve that standard of living. Foreign aid going into impoverished areas today is about 10 billion dollars or $6 per capita per year. It is estimated that government plus private investment in this country is about $9,000 per capita; that one trillion dollars of investment is needed if the goal is to raise the standard of living to only one-fourth of what it is in the European Common Market. The release of 150 billion dollars a year now spent on armament would not mean that all of it would be spent on foreign aid. If 2.6 billion people received an annual expenditure of $35 per capita, the total foreign aid going into underdeveloped nations each year would be 91 billion dollars. And $35 a year is only a start, especially if the world population growth continues at the rate of 1.7 per cent (its rate since World War II). For on that assumption we would have in eighty years (2043 A.D.) a world population of 11.7 billion as compared to our present population of 3.1 billion. President Eisenhower reduced the problem to elementary terms in a speech on April 16, 1953:

> Every gun that is fired, every warship launched, every rocket fired signifies, in the final sense, a *theft* from those who hunger and are not fed, those who are cold and are not clothed. . . .
> The cost of one modern heavy bomber is this: a modern brick school in more than thirty cities. . . .
> We pay for a single fighter plane with a half million

bushels of wheat. We pay for a single destroyer with
new homes that could have housed more than eight
thousand people. . . .

This is not a way of life at all, in any true sense.
Under the cloud of threatening war, it is humanity
hanging from a cross of iron. . . .

So, apart from the problems of nuclear war, disarmament is the world's number one concern, if mounting
population pressures alone are not to produce revolutions
of despair. For it is only through disarmament that war
can be prevented and adequate resources released for
raising the world's standard of living. Prevention of war
will be well-nigh impossible if the race to get bigger and
better stockpiles of bombs continues. There is no reason to
think that those who will rise to power in the future will be
better integrated, more stable, less aggressive than those
who rose to power in bygone days.

Even peaceful use of nuclear energy poses difficult
problems. As of 1959, the United States had 65 million
gallons of high activity radio-active water in storage. By
1980, these by-products of the peaceful use of nuclear
energy will amount to from 100 to 300 million gallons,
storage waters that will have about 10 billion curies. That
is to say, they will emit the same number of alpha rays per
unit of time as 10 billion grams of radium. These waste
products cannot be detected by human tests or odor. Their
life is long—perhaps 1,000 years, perhaps longer. Failure
to control what is stored today may lead to vast disasters
next year, or in the far distant centuries. Will concrete con-
tainers buried in the ocean last that long? What is the life
of the stainless steel that holds these wastes? Can they be
disposed of in the ionosphere? These are problems that
concern the experts. Fission by-products may be tem-

porarily disgorged in the stratosphere or sunk deep in the oceans. But they eventually return to plague the skies, the shores, and the waters of every country. As of 1963, no nation in the world has found a solution to disposal of these high level radio-active wastes. International regulatory action is necessary. Only supranational action can save all of us—white, black, brown, yellow—from the new perils generated by our scientific achievements.

A start has been made by Russia and the United States in reaching an agreement on the peaceful uses of space. Preliminary agreements looking towards the establishment of a global weather satellite system, a geomagnetic pact, and a telecommunications satellite joint experiment have been worked out. In each instance, there will be cooperation with the appropriate units of the United Nations.

The sharp cleavages that exist in the world make this a challenging task. The dictatorships of the communist world as opposed to the democracies of the West mark only some of the differences. There are absolute monarchies, dictatorships, and democracies at various stages of development. Each competes for followers. The goals and ideals are many and diverse.

Moreover, much of the world is in a *status quo* that must be changed. The *status quo* in the underdeveloped nations is mostly feudalism, which will give way before powerful forces of change. The future will therefore be turbulent, if not chaotic.

Much of the world is illiterate. Across the Middle East, in Asia, in South America, illiteracy is the rule. Leaders in these countries must make bricks without straw.

The vast gulfs that exist between various world cultures mean that the common ground will be narrow and selective. There are only limited areas where a common ground can be found. Yet they are important, indeed critical, ones; and they will expand as the peoples of the world work with their newly emerging institutions and gain confidence in them.

The small nations have as great a proclivity to lawless action as any others. Boundary disputes, fishing rights, territorial claims—all of these often take the form of ugly episodes, no matter the size of the nations involved.

Those disputes increase in intensity when ideological differences are sharp. The opposed policies of the Soviet bloc and the Free World tend to find expression in opposed laws. Where the cleavages in policy are great, *consensus* (the basis of law) will be found only in limited areas. The problem of survival is to widen the areas of *consensus*.

The search for new devices of security is not as difficult as it may seem. Various forces have long been building an international community together with a skeleton of law that supplies a degree of cohesion. Trade and commerce are developing common markets and out of them comes a new order of government. As the world is evolving there are few, if any, nations that can go it alone. None is an isolated, insulated unit. Sovereignty may in theory be entirely in local hands. Yet the very need for raw materials or food or loans or technicians from abroad creates a dependency on other nations. There are not many examples of self-sufficiency.

Technology brings all peoples closer together with new common problems to solve. One is the problem of communications, now placed in a new perspective by reason of the satellites. Two satellites (or three at most) located at a distance of 22,300 miles from the earth can contain all the electronic devices necessary for a worldwide system of communications. Through those satellites direct dialing of any telephone in the world is theoretically possible. Through them we can put colored television into Russia or into any other country. If the nations are to be bound together into worldwide systems of communications, we need multi-nation agreements even vaster in scope than those pertaining to disarmament.

The emergence of new nations has made even more urgent the need for supranational agencies. The United Nations now contains over 100 members. Centuries of colonialism have ended; nations or races long subjugated by outside regimes have gained their independence. Some are weak, inexperienced, fragile. They have come into their inheritances at a time when world forces are aligned into powerful blocs that might make them pawns in the old game of power politics.

No nation wants to become either a puppet of an imperialistic regime or a communist satellite. Those in the orbit of Moscow or Peking would rather be a Yugoslavia than a Hungary. If independence is to be kept, as well as achieved, they must have a refuge, a sanctuary where they can feel secure. The United Nations satisfies that craving for security. And its success in the Congo, in protecting a new nation from the internal machinations of foreign powers, dramatized its usefulness.

One handicap of the United Nations has been that it excluded groups that should have been included. Peking is still excluded. Yet the Peking regime, under which nearly a fourth of the people of the world live, is established more firmly than a mere *de facto* regime. Professor John Tuzo Wilson of Toronto University made startling disclosures as to Peking's progress in science.[8] We can assume she will have her own atomic warheads before long. Meanwhile she is an expansionist nation. Her tactics against India have added up to calculated aggression. Her tactics against Tibet have exceeded in ruthlessness and cruelty the actions of Russia in Hungary. Tibet—never rightfully a province of China in spite of several centuries of Chinese propaganda—has been incorporated into it.[9]

Peking is an outlaw, it is said; and being an outlaw is given as the reason for barring her from the United Nations. But in reality how can an outlaw be kept outside the United Nations and yet be disciplined by it? There is today no tribunal to which Peking can be made to account. There is no assembly or council before which she can be summoned. With Peking absent, disarmament talk is only classroom chatter.

Traditionally, "recognition" of a government did not necessarily imply approval of its regime. President Grant said in 1875 concerning the recognition of Cuba, that in such a case "other nations simply deal with an actually existing condition of things, and recognize as one of the powers of the earth that body politic which, possessing the necessary elements, has, in fact, become a new power. In a word, the creation of a new state is a fact." [10] That reflected the traditional view. The historic tests have been (1) whether a government exists independent of another state, and (2) whether it has internal stability and is a functioning government. By Jefferson's standards a government was to be recognized if it represented "the will of the nation, substantially declared." [11]

Conditions changed and the concept of "recognition" served other ends; it has at times "become a political weapon wielded to force a new government to make concessions to the demands of the recognizing state." [12] As far as precedents go, one can find what he is looking for.

But as recently stated: "In the absence of effective international guarantees for securing just government and proper administration of the law within the various States, it is impossible to insist on the perpetuation of any existing regime by a refusal to recognize its revolutionary successor. Neither is it in the long run practicable to adopt the indirect method of refusal of recognition as a means of compelling the fulfillment of international obligations. The more rational method is to grant recognition and then to insist, by such means as International Law offers, on the proper fulfillment of its obligations on the part of the recognized Government." [13]

The same approach must be taken if there is to be a real United Nations. A Free World Club, like a Communist Club, would include only like-minded nations. But the United Nations by definition is designed to cope with all the problems of a troubled and diversified world. A United Nations that is such in fact must be able to bring its influence to bear upon all world problems that affect the peace or that impair the integrity of nations.

The United Nations is far from being the Parliament of Man that Tennyson wrote about; yet it is a significant advance toward a Rule of Law in world affairs.

We have had in legal circles in the United States a narrow limited view of law. Thomas Hobbes in 1651 took what became a rather classic but restricted idea of law—that a "sovereign" is the source of all law. This meant, in Hobbes' view, that "equity, justice" or other "qualities that dispose men to peace and obedience" are "not properly laws." [14] John Austin gave the Hobbesian philosophy impetus. Several generations of American lawyers have been influenced by Austin and his book, first published in

1832, where law in the strict sense was defined as the body of rules enforced by a sovereign state.[15] World law, in that view, requires a full-fledged superstate in which all nations are merged—a supranational organization that has political and military control over all of its units. Under this view, world government would require a highly centralized organization.

A full-fledged system of world government—the one that is best thought out in terms of political theory and political reality—has been proposed by Grenville Clark and Louis B. Sohn.[16] It provides a plan, based on a revision of the Charter of the United Nations, which entails national disarmament to the police level, creation of a UN police force, creation of machinery for peaceful settlement of international disputes, abolition of the Security Council and its replacement by an Executive Council in which no member has a veto, a revenue system for the UN, establishment of a World Development Authority, restraints on the central government, and a new voting arrangement which in effect gives the balance of power in the General Assembly to the smaller nations. Recently Clark and Sohn have proposed an alternative plan which would achieve essentially the same ends through a treaty establishing a World Disarmament and World Development Organization affiliated with the United Nations. These plans have been widely circulated; and they have been translated into many foreign languages.

Debates on the merits of these proposals are almost nonexistent. How can their political need be made apparent? When will official international groups be designated to explore the common problem and report to their people? When will we and the Russians (not to mention the Chinese) awaken to the realization that each can no longer go it alone, that, like it or not, we are in the same fragile boat and desperately interdependent?

In 1962 General Eisenhower recommended the establishment of a World University to be attended by students of all nations and staffed by an international faculty, chosen by the United Nations, "whose concern would be objective truth, purged of national and regional bias, hatred and prejudices." This proposal too has been widely circulated and little debated.

To do these things is a formidable task both at home and abroad. At home it means opening up the free market of ideas that has been more and more restricted since World War II. It means reintroducing a "loyal opposition" to foreign policy and reopening foreign policy to debate. It also means matching the power of the military-industrial complex against which President Eisenhower warned in his Farewell Address.

All states, however, need not be merged in one world state, in order that their conduct may be subordinate to a Rule of Law. The true gauge of law is not command but conduct. Those who move to the measured beat of custom, mores, or community or world mandates are obeying law in a real and vivid sense of the term. Law is a force that shapes and moulds the affairs of men. The fact that there may be no court to enforce a rule of conduct does not prove that no international law exists. The most effective laws are those that spring from custom. They indeed seem more enduring than laws written on parchment. It is in this broad frame of reference that Grotius placed international law—"that body of law . . . which is concerned with the mutual relations among states or rulers of states, whether derived from nature, or established by divine ordinances, or having its origin in custom and tacit agreement." [17]

Marcus Aurelius many centuries ago stated: "If our intellectual part is common, the reason also, in respect of which we are rational beings, is common: if this is so, common also is the reason which commands us what to do, and what not to do; if this is so, there is a common law also; if this is so, we are fellow citizens; if this is so, we are members of some political community; if this is so, the world is in a manner a state." [18]

The United Nations is today the expression of world opinion that the cult or regime of force must be replaced by a measure of world law. The United Nations represents all aspects of the Rule of Law—adjudication by judges and arbiters, administrative action, executive power, and the legislative function. Yet those agencies have little on which to operate when the applicable international law is fragmentary. "The issues involved are generally not strictly legal, but political, and often relate to the problem of peaceful change for which the law provides no adequate or quick solution." [19] The Rule of Law in world affairs requires, in other words, a *legislative* function.

The Legislative Function and the U.N.

We are accustomed to think of legislation only in terms of actions of parliamentary bodies. That is one way—but only one—in which the policy of a nation is fashioned. A sovereign power announces new policies or refashions old ones by its parliaments, by its chief executive, or by agencies it has created and authorized to act. For example, under American practice national policies in the international field are formulated by the President in Executive Agreements as well as by the President and the Senate in the making of treaties. The formulation of a national policy, however it is done, is legislating in the broad sense of international law.

All law is the product of the political process. Arguments, discussions, conferences, diplomacy, resolutions of international agencies, produce for a given situation—or for a generalized problem—a rule of conduct. The political process creates an arbitral or judicial tribunal and assigns a controversy to it for adjudication. Alternately the political process recognizes an executive task and creates an administrative agency to undertake it.

The *legislative* function is expressed in the Charter of the United Nations. It is felt in the resolutions of the Security Council or the General Assembly of the United Nations. It is expressed by the Great Powers in developing "a *consensus* as to the ground rules to be observed to prevent . . . disputes from erupting into war." [20]

On June 27, 1950, when the Security Council resolved to furnish such assistance "to the Republic of Korea as may be necessary to repel the armed attack" and "to restore international peace and security in the area," forty-odd nations approved. India's views represented perhaps the common denominator of world opinion. For she stated that she was "opposed to any attempt to settle international disputes by resort to aggression." [21]

It indeed was a new principle of international law that had been forged by experience and expressed in legislative terms in the Charter of the United Nations: "to take effective collective measures for the prevention and removal of threats to the peace, and for the suppression of acts of aggression or other breaches of the peace." The United Nations' action in Korea was the first time the outlawry of aggression was implemented by direct military action by the community of nations. Aggressive war had become too dangerous to the world community to be allowed. This was noble, principled, responsible action that gave power and force to a newly forged tenet of international law.

The abstention of Russia from the Security Council when the United Nations came to the aid of South Korea and her subsequent claim that the United Nations acted unlawfully when it did so, had far-reaching consequences. On November 3, 1950, the General Assembly passed a Resolution entitled *Uniting For Peace*. By that Resolution it was decided that if the Security Council, because of lack of unanimity of the permanent members, fails to exercise its primary responsibility for the maintenance of international peace and security, the General Assembly is to consider the matter immediately. Under the terms of the Resolution the General Assembly may meet for that purpose at the request of the Security Council, if seven of the members so vote, or at the request of a majority of members of the United Nations. The General Assembly may then recommend the use of armed force, when necessary, to maintain or restore international peace or security. This Resolution is a constitutional landmark in the development of international lawmaking.[22] It did, indeed, greatly strengthen the legislative power of the United Nations.

The aftermath of the Korean issue confused the clear-cut problem before the United Nations. The Soviets soon denounced the United Nations' police action in Korea as "war"—a "war" that the United States inspired and conducted under the cloak of the United Nations. Eisenhower in his campaign speech of September 4, 1952, gave ammunition to the Soviets. He, too, called the police action in Korea a "war." The expediency of American politics caused the vital distinction between United Nations "police action" and "war" to become blurred and confused. The United States retreated temporarily from the principled decision that "aggressive war" called for world action against the aggressor.

Since those days, the world has regained some of the lost ground. On November 2, 1956, the General Assembly voted 64 to 5 for a cease-fire on the actions undertaken against Egypt. Later that month it created an international command force of the United Nations to supervise the cessation of hostilities; and in a matter of a few days hostilities ceased.

India's invasion of Goa is inexplicable except in terms of emotions run wild. According to Nehru, the popular reaction in India to the annexation of Goa was, "As if some great burden had been removed, some corroding evil had been eliminated." Indian communists had long tried to arouse public sentiment against Goa as a diversionary tactic to remove some of the embarrassment to Indian communists caused by Peking's repeated invasions of India. India's justification was that by taking Goa she broke the bonds of colonialism. The American Revolution was cited as a precedent. But the Goa incident was not a force boiling from within and overthrowing a colonial regime. It was an invasion from without. Goa had long been a political entity that existed on the border of a succession of empires—Mogul, Marathas, British. For over 450 years it was territory covered by the Portuguese flag.

Today, the use of force to gain or reclaim lost territory is not a permissible alternative. Many instrumentalities for

settling international disagreements are available. What
New Delhi says to justify Goa is what Peking will say to
justify taking Sikkim, Bhutan, and Nepal. Where the desire is strong, the rationalization comes easily. Russia gave
high-sounding security reasons for swallowing Lithuania,
Estonia, and Latvia. We live in an era where the exploits
of India in Goa, of China in India, our abortive invasion
of Cuba, England's aggression in the Suez, and Russia's
along the Baltic are beyond the pale. Force against a
neighboring nation, like force against an individual, is no
longer permissible except (a) in self-defense, or (b) in
execution of a mandate of law, such as took place in
Korea and in the Congo.

Nehru only a few years prior to the invasion of Goa had
said: "There is nothing I can argue with any person who
thinks that the methods employed in regard to Goa must
be other than peaceful, because we rule out non-peaceful
methods completely. Once we accept the position that we
can use the army for the solution of our problems, we
cannot deny the same right to other countries." [23] That is
the only permissible viewpoint in this nuclear age.

When the Republic of the Congo asked for help from
the United Nations to maintain its government against the
machinations of a foreign power, and when, in response,
the Security Council on July 13, 1960, resolved to extend
that aid, a new principle was forged. Protection of a nation
against aggression from without was extended to protection
against any form of intervention by a foreign power.

The Congo operation cost about ten million dollars a
month. The United Nations patrol along the Israeli-Egyp-
tian border cost about twenty million dollars a year. These
two operations put the United Nations in the red. Its
members who were opposed to those projects refused to

pay the special assessments necessary to maintain them. That made necessary the United Nations bond issue.

Among the nations financially in arrears with respect to the cost of operations in the Congo and Middle East were Russia, France, most of the Asian countries, most of the Latin American countries, many of the African countries, Belgium, Portugal, Italy, and Austria. Those nations argued that the special assessments were not part of the basic budget of the United Nations. The International Court of Justice ruled otherwise. It handed down an advisory opinion in 1962 declaring that the expenditures involved were regular "expenses of the organization" within the meaning of Article 17 of the United Nations Charter, and therefore must be borne by all members of the United Nations.[24]

The problem remains of financing other operations which exceed the regular budget. As of March, 1963, a U. N. Finance Committee had failed to work out a plan for financing future operations that would be acceptable to all. A majority, however, accepted most of the principles suggested; and the regular budget has been consistently met, only a few members having defaulted. Thus over-all, the nations of the world accept the United Nations as a permanent institution.

Less conspicuous *legislation,* but nonetheless important, are treaties between nations. Under the American Constitution they are part of the "supreme law" of the land that supersedes conflicting state laws. States may provide such inheritance laws as they like. But when the United States agrees with another nation that the nationals of each who die in the other nation, leaving property, heirs or next of kin abroad, shall not be discriminated against, that agreement supersedes conflicting state law.[25] The United States in an agreement with Russia took assets, located in this country, of a Russian company that had been expropriated by the Soviets. The fact that such an arrangement was void under New York law did not prevent its being a valid agreement under federal law.[26] Nations of the world subscribed to the Hague Convention which prescribes for the conduct of war the status, rights, and duties of enemy nations as well as of individuals who are enemies. The Convention supplies "the law of war" that is to be applied by each nation that is a subscriber.[27]

There have been many types of conventions touching international problems. International arrangements for copyrights and for patents also have been long standing. The arrival of the airplane brought new international conventions into existence.

Custom and usage, as well as formal agreements or conventions, state a policy that is reflected in international law. Fishing vessels may be exempt as prizes of war solely by ancient usage.[28] Custom that protects a sovereign power from suit for certain claims is recognized as international law.[29] Custom often determines the rights of aliens.[30] The three-mile belt along the seaward borders of a nation became a part of its domain by custom and usage.[31]

The question of what areas of the sea can be claimed by a nation is often vitally important. Valuable fishing rights [32] and petroleum fields [33] and other mineral claims may be involved. Usually each nation through its executive or legislative organs announces its claim. The United States, for example, has claimed nine nautical miles in the Gulf of Mexico and three geographical miles in the Atlantic and Pacific. Other nations have claimed wider zones. The Second United Nations Conference on the Law of the Sea considered various proposals, including one that would give a coastal state exclusive fishing rights for a distance of twelve miles offshore. No agreement was reached, leaving the matter to bilateral agreements between nations. Thus a recent treaty between Great Britain and Norway allows British ships to fish between six and twelve nautical miles off Norway up to October 31, 1970, but no closer than twelve nautical miles after that date.

Ad hoc arbitral tribunals have been numerous since the mid-seventeenth century.[34] The United Nations in 1958 proposed a Convention on the Recognition and Enforcement of Foreign Arbitral Awards. Though the United States has not joined it, the Convention became effective on June 7, 1959, Israel, Morocco, and the United Arab Republic having ratified it. Modern arbitration of international disputes flowered following the Jay Treaty of 1794 between the United States and England, which had an arbitration clause under which the parties submitted a boundary question. The dispute was resolved by arbitrators whose decision was "final and conclusive" as provided in the Treaty.[35] Before the nineteenth century had ended nearly 200 awards were rendered by international arbitrators adjudicating claims between different nations.[36]

Arbitration is not mediation or conciliation but a determination according to law. "In this proceeding therefore the function and duties of the Arbitrator are those of the judge, not those of the mediator; the methods and processes of decision judicial, not mediatorial. The scope and sweep of the inquiry and search, into the facts and the law, must therefore be as wide and as free as, but no wider nor freer than, judicial methods and processes permit and enjoin." [37]

The United States has extended this fostering of private

arbitration into the international sphere by a series of treaties entered into since 1946. Typically, such a treaty provides that both agreements to arbitrate and arbitration awards will be "accorded full faith and credit." [38] Such treaties are now in effect with West Germany, Greece, Ireland, Israel, Japan, and the Republic of China.

This list is only suggestive. It illustrates the many ways by which international law is brought into being. The more international the activities of a nation, the more they weave a web of international law through treaties, conventions, and custom and usage.

The Judicial Function and the U.N.

The International Court of Justice, created by the United Nations, has a permanent status. Unlike the United States Supreme Court, it has the authority to render advisory opinions. Yet only states (not individuals) may be parties before the International Court of Justice.[39] Its jurisdiction does not extend to controversies between a state and a private company; and the nation whose interests are affected by a contract which one of its companies has made with a foreign nation has no standing to invoke the jurisdiction of the Court.[40]

The disputes with which the Court deals concern the interpretation of treaties, any question of international law, and the breach of an international obligation. It also is concerned with the nature and extent of the reparation to be made for such a breach. The aim is to have such a court "that in the body as a whole the representation of the main forms of civilization and of the principal legal systems of the world should be assured." [41] Enforcement of the decrees of the Court is entrusted by the Charter of the United Nations to the Security Council.[42] Its jurisdiction to render advisory opinions may be invoked by the General Assembly or by the Security Council.[43]

The Court is an honored institution. Its judges are not mere nominees of the governments of their countries. They are nominated by national groups of jurists. No national group may nominate more than four persons, and of those four not more than two shall be of its nationality. From this list the General Assembly and the Security Council proceed independently to elect the judges. Those who obtain an absolute majority of votes both in the General Assembly and in the Security Council are elected.[44]

The Statute of the Court has several provisions to insure the independence of the judges. No member of the Court may exercise any political or administrative function or engage in any other occupation of a professional nature. Nor may he act as agent, counsel, or advocate in any case, nor take part in any decision in which he has previously participated as agent or advocate or as member of any other court or commission.

The fact that a judge is of the same nationality as one of the parties is not by reason of that fact a disqualification. Indeed, if the membership of the Court includes no judge of the nationality of one or more of the parties, the party who wants representation has a right to select an *ad hoc* judge or judges to sit in that particular case. These latter provisions have often been criticized. But in this stage of development of the world community, it might well be impossible to get a *consensus* that would disqualify a judge of the nationality of one or more of the parties.

Cases can be produced where members of the Court took a favorable attitude towards the contentions and interests of their own states or of states in similar positions.

Yet even judges from nations in the communist bloc do not produce votes that have a corresponding solidarity. Some regular judges have dissented from judgments in favor of their own nation, although an *ad hoc* judge seldom has.

The Court is a human institution, and no human institution is perfect. Over-all, the regular judges of the Court have evinced a high degree of responsibility to the world community which appointed them, and have a good record of objectivity. A critical guarantee of impartiality exists in the principle that a national of a party does not have the deciding vote. While the president of the Court can break a tie, he is denied the right to exercise that function when his state is a party.

In spite of the easy availability of the International Court and its eminent qualifications, it had only six cases to adjudicate in 1960. Low as this number is, it is the highest number the Court has had before it in any one year in a decade.

In 1961, the International Court of Justice rendered one judgment. One new adversary case was filed and one request for an advisory opinion was received. At the end of 1961 the Court's docket contained three undecided adversary cases and one advisory opinion proceeding.

Most nations give only qualified acceptances to its jurisdiction. In 1946, by adoption of the Connally Amendment the United States accepted compulsory jurisdiction except as to "matters which are essentially within the domestic jurisdiction of the United States of America *as determined by the United States of America.*" [45] The amendment was attacked as a dangerous precedent for any country seeking to sponsor the rule of law. Senator Morse said: "It is, in effect, a political veto on questions of a judicial character, and it will be instantly recognized as such by all other countries. . . . [I]n our support of the United Nations, we are committing ourselves to a very large degree to the principle that it is better to entrust these international questions to responsible international institutions. . . . If history teaches us anything, it is that if States are left to decide those questions on the basis of immediate political expediency, the result is power politics and ultimately war." [46]

This "political veto" cuts both ways: a nation that does not accept compulsory jurisdiction can, when sued, refuse to submit; on the basis of reciprocity, a state which that nation wants to sue can claim that the International Court has no jurisdiction. Bonds had been issued by Norwegian state-owned banks and sold on the French bond market. These bonds contained "gold clauses" and France and Norway had long, but futile, discussions on a diplomatic level as to the effect of these clauses. France finally sought to submit the dispute to the International Court of Justice. Norway's objection to the jurisdiction of the court because, in its opinion, the bonds presented a matter of municipal and not international law, was sustained. [47]

As Professor Louis B. Sohn recently observed: ". . . the narrowness of the United States' jurisdictional declaration constitutes an important obstacle to effective protection of American trade and business abroad. As matters pertaining to the treatment of American investments in foreign countries can be easily considered as being essentially within the jurisdiction of those countries, any claims brought by the United States on behalf of injured American investors are likely to founder on a rock of our own making." [48]

This optional clause stands in the way of the United

States exerting "its best diplomatic efforts toward the establishment of a Rule of Law which we invoke so religiously." [49] This was the theme of President Eisenhower's talk to the American Bar Association on August 29, 1960. "Are we seeking a world of law or are we seeking to find ways in which we can cater to our own views and ideas in the legal field?" [50] he asked. Yet while the President and the Attorney General took positions against the Connally Amendment, the State Department invoked it in a 1959 case involving Switzerland and the United States.[51]

The validity of the reservation of jurisdiction has not gone unchallenged. Sir Percy Spender of the International Court of Justice, dissenting in the same 1959 case, expressed the opinion that "the United States Declaration of Acceptance is, and has from its inception been null and void." [52] England, France, India, and Pakistan—which once had Connally-type reservations in their declarations accepting the jurisdiction of the International Court of Justice—have now deleted them.[53]

Allocation of waters of a river between upstream and downstream users involves intricate studies, detailed adjustments. Judges traditionally undertake the task.[54] Determination of a border may involve merely a resurvey to find old markers. But some borders, e.g., the one between India and China, have never been determined.[55] What criteria must be employed? Nehru in exchange for India's recognition of Chinese suzerainty over Tibet got Chou En-lai's promise that China would recognize the line claimed by Nehru. But the Peking government never ratified Chou En-lai's promise. That kind of controversy is subject to adjudication by tribunals. Who has actually administered the disputed area in times past? Who has collected the taxes and patrolled the region? What is the citizenship of the inhabitants? To whom have they given their allegiance? Are there natural boundaries made up of high ridges or rivers? [56] These and like standards are grist for the mills of judges who sit on boundary controversies.

Judges have often made useful inventions in boundary controversies. When the middle of a river is the boundary, does the boundary change when a violent storm carves a new channel? The authoritative answer is in the negative. But when the new channel is the product of slow change, the boundary follows the new channel. This is international law fashioned by judges seeking equitable solutions.[57]

The labors of the International Court of Justice in determining fishing rights of competing nations in coastal waters have been highly creative.[58]

In 1962, in a dispute between Cambodia and Thailand, the International Court gave fresh support to time-honored principles of boundary law. Both countries claimed the ancient temple of Preah Vihear as their own; the Cambodians argued that if the boundary line between them was found to follow the line of the natural watershed through the mountains, then the temple was on a Cambodian slope. The watershed principle was upheld as a result of which Thailand cut its trade ties with Poland because the Court was headed by a Polish judge.

Law is an instrument of justice; and common-law judges, precedent by precedent, have marked a path. Moreover, equity often liberalized what law did. English and American equity traces back to Aristotle, who said that "equity bids us to be merciful to the weakness of human nature," and that judges should individualize their decisions.

Judges or arbiters who sit in adjudication of international disputes will draw from as many diverse sources as those who settle domestic affairs. Law is versatile and inventive. It can be made to meet all exigencies that the political process has nurtured. It is as familiar to the East as to the West. The Soviets, for example, have had extensive experience with arbitration. Their arbitration tribunals process about 400,000 controversies a year between agencies of state and federal government.

The International Court of Justice is feared because of the power it has. The Court is directed by Article 38 of its statute to apply the following in reaching its decisions:

> a. international conventions, whether general or particular, establishing rules expressly recognized by the contesting states;
> b. international custom, as evidence of a general practice accepted as law;
> c. the general principles of law recognized by civilized nations;
> d. subject to the provisions of Article 59, judicial decisions and the teachings of the most highly qualified publicists of the various nations, as subsidiary means for the determination of rules of law.

The exception contained in Article 59 provides that a decision has "no binding force except between the parties and in respect of that particular case." [59]

Some critics sound the alarm when it comes to the application of "international custom" and "the general principles of law recognized by civilized nations." Do the latter, they ask, include "principles of law" of communist countries? Moreover, are the human rights, embodied in the Universal Declaration approved by the United Nations, now no longer domestic matters but a part of the body of international law which the Court may apply? Fears are expressed that they are; and Lauterpacht, once a member of the Court, is cited as an exponent of the theory.[60] Lauterpacht proposed as a matter of political philosophy that "fundamental human rights are rights superior to the law of the sovereign State." [61] But Lauterpacht knew and stated that "the Declaration does not purport to embody what civilized nations generally recognize as law." It only gives expression "to what, in the fullness of time, ought to become principles of law generally recognized and acted upon by States Members of the United Nations." [62]

The General Assembly, in various Resolutions, expresses views of policy in accord with the Universal Declaration. Yet it may not provide that the Universal Declaration is a code for the adjudication of controversies between states, since it was not intended by the parties to be legally binding. The argument is largely a tempest in a teapot because, as noted, only states may be parties before the Court.[63] It is not a tribunal that entertains complaints of individuals.

It is true that not all international law can be precisely catalogued. Some is reflected in treaties. Other parts will in time be codified. There will always be a penumbra where international law will evolve case by case. Neither we of the United States nor we of the West will be able to bend the Court to our will. Neither will other blocs. For by definition the International Court is non-aligned to power blocs. It is, however, an indispensable institution to a Rule of Law; for where there is controversy there must be a referee. If we lived in the era prior to Hiroshima, we might be able to afford the luxury of going our own way. Now that the nuclear holocaust can be instantly triggered, man's only alternative is to agree with his con-

temporaries the world over on a *consensus* that makes the
Rule of Law a reality.

The Executive Function and the U.N.

The *executive* function of the United Nations is handled
by the Secretary-General. The difficulties under which that
office has operated as a result of loosely worded or vague
directives are great. The distinction that Dag Hammarskjöld brought to the office may not yet be fully understood. As one critic rightly states: "The Secretary-General
rightly took the position in the Congo controversy at the
beginning of the Fifteenth Session of the General Assembly
that he could not perform his executive functions and
maintain the integrity of his office if his right to carry out
powers delegated to him could be thwarted, not by the
action of a responsible United Nations organ, but by the
conflicting views of Member States. It was indeed fortunate
that the Secretary-General's interpretation of the constitutional powers of his office received the overwhelming
support of the members of the General Assembly." [64]

Dag Hammarskjöld made the office of the Secretary-
General a place of high distinction. He disagreed with the
view that the United Nations merely supplied "conference
machinery" for resolving conflicts. He conceived of it as a
"dynamic instrument" by which the various nations could
not only seek reconciliation of differences but through
which they could also develop new forms of collaborative
action. Dag Hammarskjöld once commented on the executive functions of the United Nations:

> The forms used for executive action by the Security
> Council—or when the Council has not been able to reach

decisions, in some cases, by the General Assembly—are varied and are to be explained by an effort to adjust the measures to the needs of each single situation. However, some main types are recurrent. Subcommittees have been set up for fact-finding or negotiation on the spot. Missions have been placed in areas of conflict for the purpose of observation and local negotiation. Observation groups of a temporary nature have been sent out. And, finally, police forces under the aegis of the United Nations have been organized for the assistance of the governments concerned with a view to upholding the principles of the Charter. As these, or many of these, arrangements require centralized administrative measures, which cannot be performed by the Council or the General Assembly, members have to a large extent used the possibility to request the Secretary-General to perform special functions by instructing him to take the necessary executive steps for implementation of the action decided upon.[65]

Russia in 1960 proposed a revision of the *executive* branch of the United Nations. Since the United Nations is composed of nations from three blocs (the West, the communist nations, and the neutralists), Russia proposed that the *executive* branch likewise be constituted with one representative from each. The idea was not accepted; and there is much to be said against it, for efficiency is more likely to be present in a single person surrounded by a representative secretariat. But in time the views of the West may well change. For as the United Nations grows in size and more and more reflects a complex of forces, it may be that no group or bloc will be satisfied with anything less than what Russia proposed. Changing problems bring new outlooks. A United Nations dominated, for example, by one bloc exclusively might in time become intolerable for the others. The problem of finding room for conflicting ideologies in a world without war will require an inventive genius which on the legal and political level will find new devices and new institutions for the workaday world.

The Administrative Function and the U.N.

The *administrative* side of international law is carried on by many agencies. Over a dozen specialized agencies represent the United Nations. Among them are the International Labor Organization (ILO), Food and Agriculture Organization (FAO), United Nations Educational, Scientific and Cultural Organization (UNESCO), International Bank for Reconstruction and Development (World Bank), World Health Organization (WHO), and International Telecommunication Union (ITU). Each of these is in a sense a government unto itself.

ILO has nearly 100 nations as members. It has promoted in the main two ideas. First, the worker must be respected as an individual and helped in achieving a sense of responsibility. Second, collective relations between workers and employers must be harmonized through orderly means of resolving conflicts and through education. It has promoted many conventions, including the Abolition of Forced Labour Convention and the Discrimination (Employment and Occupation) Convention. It has worker trainee programs and the Expanded Program of Technical Assistance. Much vocational training has been extended under EPTA. ILO has been active in employment problems in underdeveloped nations. It has ambitious projects for the training of managers for plants in the newly emerged nations. It has been active in developing handicrafts and small-scale industries, standards for working conditions, social security, occupational safety, housing, and vocational rehabilitation.

WHO has over 100 members and each makes an annual contribution. It has launched many projects to rid areas of communicable diseases; it has helped nations acquire sanitary water supplies; it has established schools of physio-therapy in Ceylon and Pakistan; it has greatly advanced the prevention of protein malnutrition.

The United Nations also established the International Children's Emergency Fund (UNICEF) to which a hundred nations contribute. With a thirty-million-dollar budget it has launched dozens of projects both long range and emergency. Its work in Africa has been spectacular. It has put into practical application the article in the Declaration of the Rights of the Child: "Mankind owes to the child the best it has to give." [66]

The Food and Agriculture Organization is an important clearinghouse of information and a center where technical help is available. It collects world statistics on food production, international trade in agricultural products, farm prices and income, consumer prices, and agricultural credit. It surveys land reform and offers technical advisers to nations undertaking those measures. It also keeps track of the development of agricultural extension, education, and research in underdeveloped nations, and supplies technical assistance in those areas, too.

Recently, for the first time in UN history, a multi-nation conference was held at Geneva on the "Application of Science and Technology for the Benefit of the Lesser Developed Nations of the World." The conference dealt with such problems as how to overcome resistance of non-educated peoples to fertilizers, insecticides, better-balanced diets, anti-malaria and smallpox campaigns, family planning, and the acquisition of new skills in agriculture and industry. It dealt also with the problems of waste and duplication in giving technical assistance, and in pointing out areas of maximum technical aid. It tried to set general goals of an attack against poverty, hunger, illiteracy, and disease; and then to elaborate specifically on means to achieve this end.

A special report to the U. N. Economic Commission for Latin America, presented by Raul Prebish in 1963, pinpointed the problems of that feudal domain. The report emphasized that free enterprise must not be used as an excuse to maintain the existing privileged situation of a minority in Latin America. In the advanced countries, the report stated, net capital formation came first and redistribution of income later, while in the Latin American countries the two problems have to be solved simultaneously in view of the deep-seated revolutionary forces loose in the world.

The International Telecommunication Union has been widely accepted. The nations advanced in technology have indeed used it to get as many radio-frequency bands as possible. Dallas W. Smythe of the University of Illinois has reported that the "have" nations have won the radio-frequency race, the underdeveloped nations being the "have-nots" in that field also. An agency of international law becomes popular the world around once it serves many national interests.

The United Nations agencies which deal directly with problems at a "grass roots" or practical level, such as WHO, ITU, FAO, have been more immediately successful than the International Atomic Energy Agency. The potential usefulness of this agency has been frustrated by meaningless maneuvers in the cold war.[67]

The achievement of the International Bank for Reconstruction and Development, headed by Eugene A. Black, in helping to settle the Indus River dispute between Pakistan and India, is another demonstration of international law in operation. The result was the Indus Waters Treaty of 1960, whose intricate provisions are supervised by a permanent Indus Commission with provision for a Court of Arbitration to settle any differences that may arise within the Commission.

Some deride that achievement in terms of world law, saying it was only a compromise without significance. It did, however, remove from controversy a conflict over which war might have been waged. Moreover, it was a principal settlement reflecting an important rule of law. Water in one drainage area presumptively belongs to that area. Once diversions to another basin are made for the benefit of upstream users, substitute waters must be found for the benefit of downstream users. The Pakistan-India treaty is an important precedent in the common law tradition.

Ad hoc administrative instrumentalities or agencies have been created apart from the United Nations to deal with various situations.

Where self-interest is conspicuous, inventive genius finds a solution. The Danube Commission, created originally in 1856, performs strictly administrative functions and makes that river an international highway managed by the riparian states.

The International Control Commission, created in 1954 by the Geneva Conference, persuaded France and the People's Army of Vietnam to agree on a cessation of hostilities. The Commission is composed of members from Canada, India, and Poland. It served an important function in supervising the end of the war in Vietnam, and has been active in Laos.

Laos, however, teaches important lessons. Some thought they could foist a Western-oriented government on Laos. Laos—a landlocked nation next to China—offers no feasible theatre of action to the West any more than Cuba does to Russia. Laos must remain truly neutral, if it is not to be overrun by China. Russia, fearful of Chinese expansion, agreed with us in Geneva in 1961 that a neutralist government should be formed.

One sobering lesson of Laos is that if mediation or conciliation is to work successfully, there must be a *consensus*. A *consensus* could no more be reached that would plant on China's or Russia's borders a military outpost for the United States than could one by which we agreed to let a communist camp be established on our own borders.

China having long occupied Laos along with Cambodia and Vietnam, may want to put those pieces of the "mother land" back together again. The United Nations will be brought to new tests of strength once China starts to move —whether west or south. If the Peking regime is not brought within the United Nations, there is no tribunal before which she can be summoned for aggression against Laos or any other nation. It is said in reply that summoning her before the United Nations would be idle because her predatory proclivities would cause her to defy it as easily as she defies her neighbors. That is another way of saying that nothing short of a war of extermination faces the human race when the China problem is reached. Yet the Chinese, as intelligent as any other race, cannot be presumed to want national suicide. The Rule of Law, moreover, holds as much promise for one race as for another. Peking is not oblivious of world opinion. She, indeed, cultivates it as studiously as any. If she has dreams of empire, they are dreams that must be fitted into a world acutely conscious of the dangers of the nuclear age and extremely sensitive to aggression. Nations seeking friends in the forums of the world, as all peoples do, are sensitive to world opinion. The Peking regime is no exception. She enjoys a temporary immunity by being outside the United Nations. But the interest of the world community makes necessary her presence there.

The United Nations Commission for the Unification and Rehabilitation of Korea was established on October 7, 1950, by the General Assembly to stabilize conditions in Korea, to hold elections, and to unify the nation. The Commission consists of Australia, Chile, Netherlands, Pakistan, the Philippines, Thailand, and Turkey.

A proposal was made that North Korea be allowed to participate in the discussions of UNURK but without the right to vote. On December 20, 1961, the General Assembly voted 60 to 11 (with 27 abstentions) against the proposal. It was true, as stated by those opposed, that North Korea had long been recalcitrant, refusing access to United Nations bodies, and rudely denouncing United Nations authority. Yet there can be no possibility of reaching any *consensus,* if all action is to be unilateral. North Korea exists for better or for worse; she is a segment of a worrisome, difficult problem. Unless talk—patient, unhurried talk from all sides—is allowed, there is no possible way of generating the basic ingredients of any *consensus*.

There are those who say that "the best hope for peace with justice does not lie in the United Nations." They go so far as to say, "the truth is almost exactly the reverse." Their thesis is, "In our deeply divided world, peace depends on the power and unity of the Atlantic Community and on the skill of our direct diplomacy." [68]

This is talk that pleases the Pentagon, whose vested interest lies in the endless development and use of weapons. They and their counterparts in communist blocs, if uncontrolled, will trigger the holocaust. Mao Tse-tung expressed in classic form the old idea that force is essential to solve today's problems: "War is the highest form of struggle, existing ever since the emergence of private property and social classes, for settling contradictions between classes, between nations, between states, or between political groups at given stages of their development. Without understanding the circumstances of war, its characteristics, and its relation to other things, we cannot know the laws of war, cannot know how to direct it, and cannot win victory." [69]

That idea conflicts with the necessities of civilization. For the atomic age has made war a suicidal form of struggle. The only alternative we know to force is a Rule of Law: a *consensus* that produces institutions that perform the necessary legislative, judicial, executive, and administrative functions. The United Nations is not the only agency of peace in the international field. But it is indispensable. For without it there would be no international agency with the means at hand to manage acute international problems such as Korea and the Congo presented.

The United Nations must, however, be used selectively for solving problems, lest it be able to solve none. It has a unique role to fill. Originally it was conceived as an agency to keep the peace between the Great Powers. It has assumed a different task, one in many respects more difficult. That role is to help the new nations walk alone and to see to it that the underdeveloped areas can get assistance so that when they cast off the old forms of colonialism and feudalism they will avoid new oppressions. The power of the United Nations is significant when the struggles between Great Powers threaten the peace. It is not— and cannot immediately become—a cure-all. Other devices, from diplomacy to arbitration, can also be used.

The problem of our time is to think in terms of law, not of force. Submission to a Rule of Law means the abandonment of unilateral action in critical areas, lest the world go up in firestorms created by nuclear war.

FEDERALISM AND A RULE OF LAW

"Behind all national interests there is an irreducible minimum of values and aspirations which are the possessions of all mankind."

"We realize that freedom has no meaning save in the context of equality and there can be no equality without economic justice."

—SARVEPALLI RADHAKRISHNAN

WORLD PROBLEMS, like national problems, cannot always be left to a world organization for solution. Just as Washington, D. C., cannot manage local, municipal, and state affairs in the United States, so the United Nations cannot be expected to solve every world dispute. Most controversies between nations are not impregnated with danger to the world. Most of the problems that nations have in common are regional in scope, rather than worldwide. The solution or management of them requires regional compacts or arrangements. These regional agreements are, or in time will be, a type of federalism. The forms of federalism that are emerging are often more loosely organized than the original American Articles of Federation. Some may over the years evolve into over-all governmental arrangements as complete and pervasive as the United States of America. Their institutions will process and dispose of most of the international disputes that arise in the particular region, saving to all members recourse to the United Nations in case the controversy is not regionally solved.

These regional types of federalism have been emerging for a number of years. Sometimes, military compacts have provided a skeleton structure that has been incorporated into a larger non-military design.

Soviet Russia, starting with military alliances of Eastern European states, has fashioned an even broader economic and cultural community. That community has recast ancient trade routes, opened new markets, provided vast technical assistance, and trafficked heavily in cultural and ideological matters. The COMECON (Council for Mutual Economic Assistance) is the communist bloc's equivalent of the Common Market. While COMECON was originally limited to European countries, it later expanded to include Mongolia in its membership.[1]

Other regional international organizations are also organized along ideological lines. NATO is one example from the Free World. The Inner Six and the Outer Seven are another. CENTO and SEATO have their counterparts among the communist blocs of Europe and Asia.

There is a regional compact between the States of North and South America. The Charter of the Organization of American States which became effective December 13, 1951, is a legislative achievement of distinction. It provides that all international disputes between the American States shall be submitted to certain "peaceful procedures" before being referred to the Security Council of the United Nations. The procedures designated are "direct negotiation, good offices, mediation, investigation and conciliation, judicial settlement, arbitration, and those which the parties to the dispute may especially agree upon at any time." [2] OAS has as yet no Inter-American Court to adjudicate controversies between its members, though sentiment for it, originating in Ecuador, has been growing.

The parties promise in the OAS Charter not to go it alone in several respects. There is a provision that provides, "No State may use or encourage the use of coercive measures of an economic or political character in order to force the sovereign will of another State and obtain from it advantages of any kind." [3] The Charter provides a broad framework for cooperative action among the American States. Another article not only proclaims the prevention of disputes among the American States, their peaceful settlement, and common action against "aggression"; it goes further and announces that cooperative action is desired in solving "political, juridical and economic problems" arising among the American States and in promoting "by cooperative action, their economic, social, and cultural development." [4]

The Charter of OAS contains no provision for the expulsion of members. The proposal to oust Cuba, because it is a communist country, involved therefore a basic constitutional change. The adoption of that proposal at the Punta del Este Conference in 1962 established a precedent of far-reaching importance.

The OAS Charter provides that a member state may withdraw but that the Charter "shall remain in force indefinitely." [5] Amendments may be made to the Charter on two-thirds vote of the signatory states.[6] Amendments may be made to our Constitution. Would an amendment be constitutional that expelled Mississippi, New York, Vermont, from the Union?

That analogy was the stumbling block for Mexico whose

representative at Punta del Este said that in her opinion "the exclusion of a member state is not juridically possible" unless the Charter of OAS was first amended pursuant to the procedure established in the Charter.[7]

The Minister of Foreign Affairs of Brazil was also opposed to the move, saying:

> We wish to preserve and strengthen the unity of the Inter-American system and for that we consider indispensable not a unanimous and ineffective decision, but a quick and constructive solution. We wish to defend the juridical principles on which the regional system is based, and therefore we do not wish to adopt dangerous solutions that might blur the borderlines of the principle of non-intervention. Finally, we wish to fight for democracy, and therefore we wish to consider Cuba within the general framework of the antagonism between East and West, assuring conditions that will not lead to its definitive alignment with the totalitarian bloc, but that on the contrary, will give Cuba an opportunity to return, even if not immediately, to the orbit of free nations.
>
> If at this time we adopt measures that drive the country to isolation without any alternative, it cannot help but inevitably gravitate toward the Soviet bloc. On the other hand, when the Western powers have had the foresight to leave a door open, so that political, economic, and cultural contact with the West could be maintained, there has perhaps not been a single case in which the Western cause did not prevail in the end, either as to the structure of the political institutions or at least as to the definition of the state's line of international conduct.[8]

It is debatable whether the ousting of Cuba served long-range political needs of the hemisphere. The issue is so clouded with emotion that calm discussion is difficult.

There are, however, those who feel that Castro's Cuba, far removed from Russia's perimeter, would in time be as compatible with Latin America as Yugoslavia is with the European community. Moreover, those who know the quick and dramatic job Russia did in modernizing ancient Mongolia feel that like achievements can be made in Cuba in a relatively short time, provided Russia gives Cuba priority, as it seems to be doing. The vast Soviet investment in the training of thousands of Cuban farm and industrial managers is expected by some to begin to pay off shortly.

When OAS limited its membership to those nations that had comparable ideas of the Free Society, it limited its power and effectiveness. That action may have produced immediate political dividends. In the long view, the Rule of Law in world or regional affairs will suffer. The reasons why Peking should be in the United Nations are reasons why Havana should be in OAS.[9]

Cuba has long been of special concern to the United States. When John Quincy Adams was President, a proposal was made for a transfer of Cuba from Spain to France or England. Adams was opposed, and Daniel Webster supported him. Webster stated the American philosophy behind the Monroe Doctrine:

> I understood [a] member . . . to say that if Spain chose to transfer the island to any power in Europe she had a right to . . . do so, and we could not interfere to prevent it. I must, however, dissent. . . . The rights of nations, on matters of this kind, are necessarily very much modified by circumstances. Because England or France could not rightfully complain of the transfer of Florida to us, it by no means follows . . . that we could not complain of the cession of Cuba to

one of them. . . . The transfer of Florida to us was not dangerous to the safety of either of those nations, nor fatal to any of their great and essential interests. Proximity of position, neighborhood, whatever augments the power of injuring and annoying, very properly belong to the consideration of all cases of this kind. . . . The greater or less facility of access itself is of consideration in such questions, because it brings, or may bring, weighty consequences with it. It justifies, for these reasons, and on these grounds, what otherwise might never be thought of. (Reg. Debates in Cong. 19th Cong. 1st Sess., Vol. 2, Pt. 2, p. 2271.)

Opposition to the presence of Russian offensive weapons in Cuba reflected the same point of view. Russia under pressure acquiesced. Opposition to the presence of even Russian military missions and Russian defensive weapons in Cuba mounts; and some would risk war to get them out. But war with Russia means thermonuclear war, and therefore no nation capable of waging that kind of war should be driven into a corner. Unilateral action is therefore dangerous.

The three Great Powers emerging from today's realignment are the Soviet Union, the Peking regime, and the United States. Each has areas where its vital interests become quickly imperiled on the arrival of foreign troops. Russia's main area is the Middle East where Turkey stands guard over the Dardanelles; and Iran, rich in oil, offers warm water ports in the Persian Gulf. Molotov's message to Shulenburg, the German Ambassador to Moscow, dated November 25, 1940—the document that sparked Hitler's invasion of Russia—described as follows the zones of vital interest to the Soviets:

. . . the area south of Batum and Baku in the general direction of the Persian Gulf is recognized as the center of the aspirations of the Soviet Union.

It also stated:

> . . . the draft of the protocol or agreement between Germany, Italy, and the Soviet Union with respect to Turkey should be amended so as to guarantee a base for light naval and land forces of the U.S.S.R. by means of a long-term lease, including—in case Turkey declares herself willing to join the Four Power Pact—a guarantee of the independence and of the territory of Turkey by the three countries named. . . . in case Turkey refuses to join the Four Powers, Germany, Italy, and the Soviet Union agree to work out and to carry through the required military and diplomatic measures, and a separate agreement to this effect should be concluded.

The border areas of the Peking regime (which include Laos and Vietnam) are part of its sensitive zone.

If either the Soviet Union or the Peking regime protests the presence of Western troops in her vital area, she speaks in terms that are but echoes of the idea behind our own Monroe Doctrine. What Cuba is to us, Laos is to the Peking regime and Turkey and Iran are to the Soviet Union. We could no more justify unilateral action in Laos than the Soviet Union could in Cuba. Until there is disarmament, avoidance of the nuclear holocaust means a *consensus* among the Great Powers that will eliminate or reduce friction or clashes in these sensitive areas that could trigger a thermonuclear war. Unilateral action by any one of the three Great Powers makes the entire world walk the treacherous brink. Cuba and Laos illustrate the problem. No one nation can have its way. The arrival of the nuclear age has made compromise, collaboration, and *consensus* indispensable, no matter how invidious the opposed ideologies may seem to the competitors.

The European Convention for the Protection of Human Rights and Fundamental Freedoms is a regional arrangement that creates a selective administrative and judicial system.[10] It came into force in 1953; fourteen out of fifteen countries that are members of the Council of Europe have ratified it.[11] The Convention establishes a bill of rights for nationals of the member nations. It protects a wide range of human rights: "No one shall be subject to torture or to inhuman or degrading treatment or punishment." "No one shall be held in slavery or servitude." "Everyone has the right to liberty and security of person." Everyone arrested "shall be informed promptly in a language which he understands, of the reasons for his arrest and of any charge against him." Everyone arrested "shall be brought promptly" before a magistrate; one who is arrested or detained is entitled to have the lawfulness of the action decided "speedily by a court"; the victim of an unlawful arrest or detention has "an enforceable right to compensation." One charged with a crime is presumed innocent until proved guilty according to law. Punishment under *ex post facto* laws is barred. One charged with crime can have a lawyer of his own choosing, or if he is impecunious, legal representation is to be given free "when the interests of justice so require."

"Everyone has the right to respect for his private and family life, his home and his correspondence." "Everyone has the right to freedom of peaceful assembly and to freedom of association with others, including the right to form and to join trade unions for the protection of his interests." [12] Some of these rights are qualified but none may be denied on the ground of sex, race, color, language, religion, political or other opinion, etc.

The Convention establishes a Commission of Human Rights that may receive complaints from individuals or groups or from member nations, and a Court of Human Rights. The Commission deals with complaints only "after all domestic remedies have been exhausted." It makes an investigation and seeks to secure "a friendly settlement" on the basis of the rights defined in the Convention. If it is unable to effect a settlement, it reports the matter to the Committee of Ministers.

The Committee of Ministers will make the final decision, unless the case is referred to the Court within three months. A case can be referred to the Court by the Commission, the state whose national is alleged to be the victim, the member state that referred the matter to the Commission, or the member state against whom the complaint has been lodged. The Court is empowered to decide its jurisdiction should that be challenged. Its rulings on the merits involve construction of the provisions of the Convention. Its judgments are final.

The Court has had few cases to date. The Commission, however, has been busy.[13] Some complaints are from individuals who protest the action that their own government has taken against them; others are by aliens against another government. The most publicized have been those by the German Communist Party and by German Communists detained by West Germany or convicted by its courts.[14] And perhaps the most common ground for rejection of the complaints is a failure to exhaust "domestic remedies" that were available.

This Convention, designed to enforce human rights as between nations having "a common heritage of political traditions, ideals, freedom, and the rule of law," places a new and important field under international management.

The idea of the common market—which exists in the United States as a result of vigilant and liberal construction of the Commerce Clause by the courts beginning with John Marshall—has taken wings. There are several common markets in the making; and the Inner Six and Outer Seven of Europe have succeeded beyond the brightest hopes. Each common market necessarily brings into play at least a partial or skeleton form of a supranational regime.

The Court of Justice of the European Communities, which formerly adjudicated controversies in the European Coal and Steel Community, now has jurisdiction over the European Economic Community and the European Atomic Energy Community as well.[15] This Court was set up "to ensure the rule of law" in interpreting and applying the treaties. Below it are administrative commissions that issue licenses, hear complaints, make adjudications, etc. The Court adjudicates controversies between member states; but under some circumstances individuals or "legal entities" can invoke its appellate jurisdiction, as for example, to review adverse decisions by one of the administrative commissions.[16] It has been an extremely active agency in defining prohibited discriminatory practices, fixing maximum prices, helping non-competitive producers to achieve competitive positions, and restraining anti-monopoly practices.[17] It has drawn heavily upon American precedents that outlaw practices discriminatory against interstate commerce and unreasonable restraints of trade.

The Court of Justice of the European Communities is composed of seven judges, chosen for a term of years.

Some felt that no judge would rule against his own nation, or if he dared do so, that he would not be renamed to the Court when his term expired. So the practice developed of having every opinion *per curiam,* the author not being disclosed. It was also agreed that no dissents would be written or even noted. By these devices the judges acquired stature and independence that otherwise might not have arrived so early in the life of the new institution.

Regional compacts will grow. Some, starting with matters of defense, will move forward into broader fields such as the common market. There seems indeed no realistic alternative to regional compacts to satisfy regional needs. Malaysia is the start of one. It represents a federation of Malaya, Singapore, Sarawak, North Borneo, and Brunei —a total of seven million people. Though it has a heavy Chinese component, the Browns outnumber the Yellows. It puts together scattered kingdoms that could be easily infiltrated and taken over by communists, one by one. Together those states have uncommon strength and power. Malaysia may be the beginning of significant events. The larger nations of Asia—Japan, India, Pakistan, Malaysia, and the Philippines—will in time find common ground in a regional compact. One objective will be to counterbalance the massive power of Peking. Another will be to develop a common market. A third will be to render technical assistance to needy local units and to manage a continuous cultural exchange.

The nations of the Middle East—from Afghanistan to Turkey—will in time realize their common interest in protecting themselves from the designs of Russia and in freeing themselves of Western military pacts. They will eventually form a regional compact aimed at the common defense and the preservation of neutrality. Out of that arrangement an Era of Enlightenment may come to an area long plagued with invaders and colonial powers— an Era marked by vast internal reforms financed by the riches of the oil fields.

Africa, too, will doubtless move into a federation designed not so much for defense as for the pooling of purchasing power and talents for massive programs of reconstruction and for the protection of human rights.

Already twenty African nations are moving in this direction, and more will probably join them. The signing of the Lagos Charter in 1962 created OAMS (Organization of African and Malagasy States). The objectives of the Charter include mutual defense, a common attitude on foreign affairs, and broad economic links.

In Central America there is much sentiment for a Common Market. Five Central American states, Costa Rica, El Salvador, Guatemala, Honduras, and Nicaragua, plan to have by 1966 no tariffs against each other and common tariffs against outsiders. Argentina, Bolivia, Brazil, Chile, Mexico, Paraguay, Peru, and Uruguay have been negotiating a Common Market to be effective in the early 1970s.

These regional arrangements will not displace the United Nations. They will have somewhat the relation to it that states in a federal system have to the center. They will manage disputes that have no emanations beyond the particular region. They will provide the *consensus* by which regional affairs will be managed—whether in terms of a common market, defense, or the vindication of human rights.

The failure of the West and of Asia to encourage and develop regional solutions to problems of security has had dire consequences. Following World War II, the main emphasis of security measures in Southeast Asia was on

SEATO, dominated by Western powers. This led the people and governments of those countries to look to the West for help, rather than to themselves and their neighbors. The answer to the problems of insecurity largely lay, however, in measures of an internal nature.

A chapter in Malaya's history and another from Greece are illustrative.

In 1952, I traveled the back country of Malaya and saw a nation being terrorized by communist guerillas who after their raids found refuge in a jungle impenetrable except to the expert. Individual farmers had no alternative but to give the guerillas food; the terror of living in isolation in guerilla-infested areas made villagers the unwilling tools for guerilla operations. The problem was greatly eased by moving villagers into stockades at nighttime and by arming the stockades with militia.

In the late 1940s, communist guerillas roamed Greece. They would enter a village, hang the mayor and other officials, and defy the central authorities. They even raided villages to kidnap children whom they held as hostages. There was no way of calling the police, as the Greek countryside was not organized to combat guerilla tactics. The army could not be everywhere. As the guerillas struck in village after village, terror spread and people fled to large cities where they had neither food, nor work, nor lodgings. This I saw with my own eyes as I roamed Macedonia. One major problem of the American military mission was to train democratic *cadres* to fight their communist counterparts at the village level. The countryside was reinforced with gendarmes. Once people knew there were gendarmes to respond to calls for help, resistance to the communist guerillas increased.

The same phenomenon of terror grew in South Vietnam

in the late 1950s and early 1960s. Nearly thirty thousand guerillas from the north roamed the countryside, spreading terror. But Vietnamese villages had not been organized and trained in the art of countering communist guerilla tactics. By the early 1960s the American military mission in Vietnam was doing what had earlier been done in Greece. At long last village after village was trained to defend itself against guerillas. Moreover, Malaya's experience was drawn upon in building village defenses in stockades. Barbed wire and bamboo were used to encircle groups of villages, some perimeters being seven miles or more long. Along these perimeters are concrete watchtowers and pits whose bottoms are lined with upright, sharpened bamboo stakes. Thus internal security measures removed the terror that fills the hearts of a people when they know that there is no policeman they can call.

No outside power can defend another nation against guerilla infiltration. Resistance must come from within the nation itself. The image of SEATO therefore weakened rather than strengthened the cause of the Free Society.

There were eight nations in SEATO. Only three of them, Pakistan, the Philippines, and Thailand, can be called Asian. The other members are white and non-Asian —Australia, England, France, New Zealand, and the United States. Thus, SEATO perpetuated the image of Rudyard Kipling. The people of Asia are mostly colored people whose memories of their white overlords are not cherished. White armies are not welcome there. The day of the white man's domination has passed. With it SEATO too must pass for it in fact represents hardly anything more than American military might.

The prospect of regional groupings raises large problems for the world. Russia with her command over a large share of the world's riches is one of the "have" nations. The United States and the Atlantic Community are others. If both the communist bloc and the Free World bloc are to be a closed economic community, the "have-not" nations outside that community will experience a continuously worsening condition. The new industries going up in underdeveloped nations will be high-cost producers, as compared with the established ones. If the rich markets are closed to them, the gap between the millionaires and the starving peons will in the near future produce many revolutions. If the revolutions that gave birth to the new nations result only in a greater disparity between the "haves" and the "have-nots," the world will be torn asunder.

Today the collective national income in the underdeveloped nations is somewhere in the neighborhood of $135 billion annually. American national income alone is nearly $450 billion. The Western world that has a population of about 400 million people has a collective income of about $1,000 billion annually. When the Western income mounts, as it will, the discrepancy with the "have-nots" will increase. If that happens *without marked growth of national income in the underdeveloped areas,* despair in those regions may take on violent revolutionary aspects.

This brings us back to the problem of the common market, already mentioned. We of the West must not seek refuge in closed societies and common markets that exclude the "have-nots." Moreover, we should make room in our preferential trade groupings for nations who fear to become locked into a communist bloc.

A nation left out of the European Common Market may suffer Iceland's fate. That nation of 170,000 people has as its main export fish fillets. In 1960 she sold 36,000 tons to the Soviet Union because she could not obtain acceptable prices from the European Community. As a consequence, over 90 per cent of her oil comes from Russia; and much of her motor cars, machine tools, ships and other industrial products come either from Russia or the communist bloc.

The pressure of Europe's Common Market on Latin America is already apparent. Temperate zone products, such as meat, are hard hit. So are tropical products—coffee, bananas, and cocoa. Latin America in order to survive is begininng to look more and more to the Soviet bloc. There is unfolding before our eyes the ominous role that trade can play in political infiltration.

Finland was heavily loaded with reparations by Russia at the end of World War II and was required to build a steel plant through which payments would be made. But it was and is a high-cost mill unable to compete on the world market, and probably the only common market into which it could fit would be one of the communist bloc. Yet if the rest of Finland's trade is not admitted to the common markets of the Free World, the communist economic noose may eventually strangle her. Trade is a potent weapon. In 1962 some 30 per cent of the COMECON trade was external.[18]

Even countries in the communist bloc should not be closed out. Poland, largely dependent for Western currencies on her exports of pork, needs that trade if even a degree of independence from the communist bloc is to be achieved. Eastern European nations in COMECON fear becoming locked too tightly into it. For their fate may then be that of nations under colonial regimes. Rumania has recently protested becoming a supplier of raw materials to Russia's industrial plant. That was Yugoslavia's earlier protest—the reason she broke with Russia in 1948. Yugoslavia, a communist nation that is far to Russia's right and passionately independent in spirit, needs continuous access to the markets of the Free Society.

The new United States Trade Act which forbids the most-favored-nation treatment to "any country or area dominated or controlled by communism" does a disservice to those nations which, though communist, are evolving more benign systems. It also does disservice to the cause of the Free World, whose interests and security lie in fragmentation of communist blocs rather than in the growth of solidarity.

Trade is an ideological weapon and as effectively usable by the Free Society as by the communist bloc. Debates over the common market in any one country naturally reflect the self-interests of its people. But in the long view the interests of the "have-not" nations must also be considered, as well as the interests of those who, though communist, want to escape utter dependence on Moscow or Peking. Unless those considerations shape our policies, two equally disastrous results will follow: the rich will get richer [19] and the hold of the communist bloc on nations within its trade zones will become tighter.

Today all humanity is tied irrevocably together in an effort to escape the nuclear holocaust, to survive, to make technology the servant. The scientific revolution reaches all nations—the West and the communist bloc, as well as the "have-nots." The speed and quality differ, region to region; but the over-all effect is to make us all partners in irreversible revolutionary trends. The unemployment in India, due to underdevelopment, is matched by growing unemployment in industrialized societies due to automation. The revolutions that operate at differing levels on each continent will require adaptations of which we may not even be conscious today. They require bold planning and adventurous thinking. They mean we must make a continuous search for the common denominator in all humanity, so that bridges of understanding and cooperation can be built.

The tools with which the nations of the world can evolve a Rule of Law into a more mature system are at hand. Only the will to use them is lacking. Why do nations hold back? Why are they not willing to inaugurate a truly golden age for international law? World opinion is ready to be marshaled. Small nations quiver on the sidelines as they watch giant rivals spar, threaten, and shake their nuclear fists. The world is filled with such a sense of insecurity that for the first time in history solid foundations for a Rule of Law can be laid.

The fashioning of a Rule of Law for a troubled area takes time and patience and the realization that a *consensus* is necessary if the nuclear holocaust is to be avoided. No major breakthrough in international law has been achieved easily. Ideas of sovereignty and self-sufficiency do not slough off readily. It took the tragic years of the League of Nations and another war to prepare the world for the United Nations. It took years to achieve a peace treaty that established the modern Austria. Even the evolution of the European Common Market required painful reconciliations:

> France wanted to be sure that her more generous scale for overtime pay and her more rigid adherence to the principle of equal pay for men and women would not handicap her industries in the free trade of the Common Market.

Italy wanted to be certain that her efforts to industrialize would not be swamped by the superior industrial machines of Germany and the other member countries.

West Germany had to be assured that her high-cost agriculture would not be inundated under a flood of low-cost Dutch and French products.

The Benelux countries wanted to maintain their ability to purchase raw materials and semifinished goods for their processing industries at low world market prices.[20]

France's rejection of Great Britain as a member of the European Common Market is living evidence that old fears, ancient prejudices, and long-standing suspicions die slowly.

The system of world law, with a universal parliament of men, is far distant. What shape it will take, no one is wise enough to know. The more intensive the exploration, the more often the discussions, the better the chance of evolving it. Meanwhile problems press for solution; conflicts arise; tensions grow; and in some areas relations between nations fester. These day-to-day crises need settlement. This generation can accelerate the pace of development towards a Rule of Law—both at the regional and world levels—by using existing or newly invented procedural devices to settle the minor and major conflicts between nations.

G. B. Chisholm, the distinguished Canadian psychiatrist, spoke of the many deterrents at work among us that make us prone to leave the big problems of society to others to solve. We get a fleeting sense of social responsibility by writing a letter to our Congressmen. But as Chisholm said:

If now we all revert to our little private concerns, if we all tell ourselves "it is someone else's responsibility,"

there will one day be none of us left, not even any to
bury the dead.[21]

One who undertakes a program of this nature meets
at once formidable obstacles. The word "peace" has become almost subversive to some. Those whose business
is dependent on the Pentagon's *largesse* look with mis-
givings on disarmament. Some communities are so dependent on military projects that "peace" to them means
another great depression. Much planning is of course
necessary to replace the bounties which the war economy
have made popular. Yet no degree of planning will be
adequate unless the mood of the day changes. The United
Nations to some is only an instrument to employ against
the undesirables. In truth, however, it provides the basic
structure under which the multi-ideological world can
begin to solve its problems. We know from our own experience in federalism that no union endures when some
of the states are above the law and can defy the federal
regime. The United Nations is not as far advanced as our
federal system; it is only embryonic. Yet it has institutions
through which many of the world's clashes and contests
can be peacefully resolved.

Mr. Justice Holmes once said, "Universal distrust
creates universal incompetence." [22]

Familiarity does not always breed contempt. Nations—
now forced to live together in spite of their ideological
differences—can find their places in the sun under a Rule
of Law. No nation can expect to have its way all the time
by bending an international organization to its will. No
international organization can be used as a hammer by any
Great Power to crush the opposition.

Most of the brains—East and West—are still preoccupied with military solutions. The Russians concentrate on the difference between world war, local war, liberation war, and popular uprisings. Members of the Foreign Policy Research Institute of the University of Pennsylvania announced [23] in 1962:

> . . . the strategy of *win strike second,* is our current official position. We make our bid to win after we have absorbed the Soviet Union's first strike. Thus, we must strike back with counterforce; hold Communist bloc cities in hostage; mobilize what is left of our nation; free our allies and the satellites; and seize and occupy the Soviet Union and Red China.
>
> This is the ideal American strategy.

Or as another group has said:

> Our strategy need not include bypassing the State Department, or breaking diplomatic relations with the Soviets, or quitting the U. N. Indeed, diplomacy will remain one of our major weapons in this struggle. But like so many other elements of our present policy, diplomacy needs to be told its objective. Strausz-Hupe, Kintner and Possony thus define that objective: to make Communism "yield its stranglehold on its own peoples, turn its back on its designs for world conquest and, ultimately, surrender its power to a successor government responsive to legitimate Russian aspirations." Our objective could also be stated as Lincoln stated his policy with respect to slavery: to put armed Communism where "the public mind will rest in the belief that it is in the course of ultimate extinction." [24]

These views, backed by the Pentagon's billions, project the central problem of the age in military terms. Certainly if the Free World were unilaterally disarmed, it would be overrun. But the projection of our force into communist territories, as one group endorses, like reliance on nuclear power, as the other group proposes, makes more certain the triggering of the holocaust. Communism will run its course. Belgrade is as far to the right of Moscow as Moscow is to the right of Peking. Once the Russian armies are withdrawn from Eastern Europe, there will be a flowering in some countries that will also put them far to the right of Russia. Russia itself will soon be an affluent society, more interested in internal contentment than external aggression. Time will soften the clashes between the Western world and the communist bloc as it did between Christianity and Islam.

All of mankind is now the smallest community in the world. Whether we like it or not, a world that can be circled in an hour is One World. Mankind can no longer be thought of as "divided into opposed species." [25] The concept of the "good and the bad," "we and they," that has dominated the human race from the beginning spells doomsday when it is projected into the nuclear age. "If the world is divided between the good and the wicked, then the triumph of the good implies the destruction of the wicked. 'The only good Indian,' said the North American pioneer, 'is a dead Indian.' . . . [S]o the Nazi regime in Germany undertook the extermination of Jews; so we Americans were able in 1945 to destroy the people of Hiroshima and Nagasaki." [26]

As the wife of an American Ambassador in Southeast Asia recently said to me, "There is too much we-ness versus they-ness in the world. We are the 'good'; they are the 'bad'; just like cats are 'good' and mice are 'bad.' We need to educate ourselves to the oneness of mankind."

The philosophy of the American Declaration of Independence, as summed up by Carl Becker, today expresses a universal yearning among men: "At its best it preached toleration in place of persecution, good-will in place of hate, peace in place of war. It taught that beneath all local and temporary diversity, beneath the superficial traits and talents that distinguish men and nations, all men are equal in the possession of a common humanity; and to the end that concord might prevail on the earth instead of strife, it invited men to promote in themselves the humanity which bound them to their fellows, and to shape their conduct and their institutions in harmony with it." [27]

The immediate problem is to understand each other— the peoples of the world—as members of one race. It is easy to search the world for characteristics that make people ugly. Our search must be for qualities that make people warm-hearted though frightened, noble though hungry, idealistic though illiterate, cooperative although ideologically different.

Nationalism often accentuates the difference. The color line whips up passions and may even give the cast of a paranoid to a community. Trade barriers can create animosities as deep as ideological cleavages.

The burden of building a world without war is freighted with difficulties. But there are no other alternatives. The problem is to find piece by piece the things that all peoples have in common and to build common aspirations and endeavors around them.

Dual citizenship is a version of world citizenship; and the realization that each of us is a citizen of the world with reciprocal rights and duties would put all current problems in a new dimension.

Hunger is one bond. Would not an offer to feed starving Chinese under the Peking regime be likely to erect some of the pillars of the new bridge of understanding that must be created between the Whites and the Yellows?

Medical care is another common link. Corps of doctors and nurses entering a benighted region to establish first aid stations, to train nurses, and to establish a medical school are emissaries who carry messages of good will.

Teachers from the West, who speak the local language, come with keys to knowledge for which there is an astronomical demand. Those who come on that mission establish enduring bonds between two nations.

Technicians who introduce seed selection may be more blessed than those who introduce electricity.

Musicians, dancers, poets, artists are members of a world-wide fraternity. The same can be said in part for lawyers and psychiatrists.

Grenville Clark has discussed the need for professional and technical training of indigenous personnel in the nations where 2.6 billion people will live in dire need. He estimates that three million young men and women in those areas will have to be trained in the numerous skills necessary for the creation and management of a modern society. Even this figure would amount only to one out of every 866 people in those low-income areas. Whether three million or six million are needed, the educational challenge is great. Societies of the West that furnish the teachers for these purposes will have built important bridges between them and the new societies of Asia, Africa, and Latin America.

Heretofore we have been mostly identified with military missions. "Will you align with us in a military pact? If so, we will help your poor and needy. If not, we will be less generous."

Heretofore we have been identified with grants or loans to help establish abroad the "free enterprise" system and the "American market system." We have in effect stated, "Create your new society in our image and we will be generous. Follow the socialist line and we will not be." The so-called Clay Report of March 20, 1963 on foreign aid indeed stated, "We believe the U. S. should not aid a foreign government in projects establishing government-owned industrial and commercial enterprises which compete with existing private endeavors."

As Professor Dallas W. Smythe of Illinois recently said, "Billions for defense but not a cent for socialism. It is not socialism to have the government spend $50 billion for weapons; it would be socialism if the government spent the same amount for education or for public works."

Thus we have made subservience to our ideology a condition of our aid. This has made us seem callous and cold to human needs, not warm-hearted and understanding. Other nations, notably Russia, that attached similar express or implied conditions also have appeared to be cold and callous. The cold war has indeed made foreign aid largely a political rather than a humanitarian term. That is essentially why many, including Paul Hoffman, believe that foreign aid should be administered through the United Nations and thus be free of entanglements of foreign policy and the cold war.

Are we mature enough to take that step? Can we be educated to the view that our true strength is in America the teacher, America the engineer, America the doctor?

The split-level house next to the country club has expressed our ideal. The affluent society has surfeited us with material things; it has indeed given us material values. Yet the world's need is different—the need is for projects that implicate the world community in common endeavors. Ernest Cuneo has shown in *Science and History* that conventional ideas of sovereignty do not fit modern needs. As he puts it, the "present problem is not one of static coexistence, but one of joint dynamic coevolution." Nation states are necessary in the evolutionary scheme. They are to a people what an integrated personality is to the individual. But the nation state is obsolete, measured by political needs of the world. There can in the long run be no salvation from nuclear ruin unless the clash of opposed forces is avoided. That can happen only by a *consensus* that produces disarmament and that establishes a supranational regime to make it effective.

Freud said:

> . . . men are not gentle, friendly creatures wishing for love, who simply defend themselves if they are attacked, but a powerful measure of desire for aggression has to be reckoned as part of their instinctual endowment.[28]

Thus our problem does not end with disarmament. The arrival of that epoch merely gives us a chance to resolve the ancient conflicts without causing a planetary disaster. The world community will need police as do communities the world over. The task of our generation is to educate the peoples of the earth on the needs of that new community and the ways and means of survival.

Those who support the traditions of the Free Society have a special role to play in promoting the conditions that make the Rule of Law a way of life. First, they can create a powerful moral force in the world by using presently existing institutions to settle their disputes. And if no institutions are adequate, they should be the first to propose the invention of new ones or the refashioning of old ones. World opinion on the side of the Rule of Law can become as strong a deterrent as bombs and armies.

Second, we need to work for a Grand Alliance with Russia, basing it at first on a *consensus* that provides the ground rules for avoidance of military clashes. From that we must move towards finding, area by area, problem by problem, practical adjustments of tensions and conflict. This process, slow and painful as it is, can succeed only as mutual suspicion wanes and mutual confidence grows.

Third, we need to intensify the search for a political *consensus* with the Soviet-Sino bloc. No quick, easy solution is likely. A continuous interchange of views, conferences and seminars, discussions and reports is essential, even to the point of replacing one group of worn-out negotiators with another. An International Rule of Law Year should be launched. The inventive genius of scholars in the West, in Eastern Europe, in Soviet Russia, and on the other continents is so great that even in troubled areas like Berlin the achievements of an International Rule of Law Year may equal those of the International Geophysical Year.

Not every matter in the life of an individual or in the affairs of a nation is negotiable. But most of them are; and enough of them must become so, if the peoples who inhabit the planet at this point are to have a chance to find a modicum of the good life.

The anatomy of liberty in this nuclear age includes the structure of the world, the relations of the peoples of the various continents to each other, and the way in which regional problems are managed. One's liberty at the community level, no matter how perfect it may seem to be at present, would disappear with a nuclear war. Devastation would be so complete that military rule would replace even the Free Society. Those left would then start anew their search for liberty. But they would struggle under conditions vastly more difficult than faced Mousterian man when he first emerged from the caves in paleolithic time.

If liberty is to flourish from this time on, man must make the Rule of Law in world, in regional, and in community affairs his preoccupation.

NOTES

CHAPTER I

1. *Thomas* v. *Collins,* 323 U. S. 516 (1944).

2. Charles Malik, in *Summary Record,* United Nations Economic and Social Council, Commission on Human Rights, February 5, 1947, pp. 3, 4.

3. Law on Organization of Special Court and Special Prosecution Division, Republic of Korea, Law No. 567, December 30, 1960.

4. Law Concerning the Organization of the Revolutionary Court and the Revolutionary Prosecution Division of the Republic of Korea, Law No. 630, June 21, 1961.

5. Law on the Punishment of Persons Involved in Unjust Elections, Law No. 586, Republic of Korea, December 31, 1960.

6. The Illicit Fortune Disposition Law of the Republic of Korea, Law No. 623, June 15, 1961 (as amended July 7, 1961; October 26, 1961; November 20, 1961).

7. Law on Restriction of Civil Rights of Persons Who Committed Anti-Democratic Acts, Law No. 587, Republic of Korea, December 31, 1960.

8. *United States* v. *Lovett,* 328 U. S. 303 (1946).

9. *Torcaso* v. *Watkins,* 367 U. S. 488 (1961).

10. Thomas Jefferson, "A Bill for Establishing Religious Freedom" (1779), in *The Complete Jefferson,* assembled by Saul K. Padover (1943).

11. J. S. Mill, "On Liberty," in Chas. W. Eliot, ed., 25 *Harvard Classics* 211 (1910).

12. *Farmers Union* v. *WDAY,* 360 U. S. 525 (1959).

13. *Baumgartner* v. *United States,* 322 U. S. 665, 673-674 (1944).

14. *Tracy* v. *Kline & Son,* 274 App. Div. 149 (1948).

15. *Dennis* v. *United States,* 341 U. S. 494 (1951).

16. *Scales* v. *United States,* 367 U. S. 203 (1960).

17. Anti-Communist Law. Republic of Korea, Law No. 643, July 3, 1961; in *Report of the United Nations Commission for the*

Unification and Rehabilitation of Korea. General Assembly: 16th Session, Supp. No. 13 (A/4900).

18. *Meyer* v. *Nebraska,* 262 U. S. 390 (1923).

19. Oppenheimer, American Association for Advancement of Science: Symposium No. 56 (1959).

20. *Thomas* v. *Collins,* 323 U. S. 516 (1944).

21. Law for the Purification of Political Activities, Republic of Korea, Art. 3, Art. 11.

22. *De Jonge* v. *Oregon,* 299 U. S. 353 (1937). For a discussion of the right of association, which is now a part of the bundle of rights protected by the First Amendment, see *Gibson* v. *Florida Legislative Comm.,* 372 U. S. 539, and *idem* at 559-576 (concurring opinion).

23. John Milton, *Areopagitica* (1644), in R. M. Hutchins, ed., 32 *Great Books of the Western World* 384 (1952).

24. The Minnesota case is *Near* v. *Minnesota,* 283 U. S. 697. The more recent Rhode Island case is *Bantam Books* v. *Sullivan,* 372 U. S. 58.

25. See: *Mutual Film* v. *Ohio Industrial Commission,* 236 U. S. 230 (1915).

26. *Joseph Burstyn, Inc.* v. *Wilson,* 343 U. S. 495 (1952).

27. *Times Film Corporation* v. *Chicago,* 365 U. S. 43 (1961).

28. *Grosjean* v. *American Press Co.,* 297 U. S. 233 (1935).

29. Roderick MacFarquhar, ed., *The Hundred Flowers Campaign and the Chinese Intellectuals.* Praeger, New York (1960).

30. Yevgeny Yevtushenko, *Stantzia Zima,* quoted in "A Soviet Poet as Rebel," *The New Republic,* January 8, 1962.

31. Yevgeny Yevtushenko, "Babi Yar," *Lituraturnaya Gazeta,* Sept. 19, p. 4 (Russian); *The Current Digest of the Soviet Press,* Vol. VIII, No. 36, p. 18 (English translation).

32. Yevgeny Yevtushenko, *op cit., supra,* note 30.

33. Gandhi, quoted in *India News,* April 27, 1962, p. 1, col. 2-3. Information Service of India, Indian Embassy, Washington, D. C.

34. James Madison, *Memorial and Remonstrance Against Religious Assessments,* in Gaillard Hunt, ed., *The Writings of James Madison,* Vol. II at 184-185; at 185; at 186; at 188. The Knickerbocker Press (1901).

35. *Everson* v. *Board of Education,* 330 U. S. 1, at 15, 16 (1947); *Engel et al.* v. *Vitale et al.,* 370 U. S. 421 (1962).

36. See: *United States* v. *Ballard,* 322 U. S. 78 (1944).

37. *West Virginia Board of Education* v. *Barnette,* 319 U. S. 624 (1943).

38. *Niemotko* v. *Maryland,* 340 U. S. 268 (1950).

39. *Murdock* v. *Pennsylvania,* 319 U. S. 105, 108, 112 (1943).

40. *Martin* v. *Struthers,* 319 U. S. 141 (1943).

41. *Jones* v. *Opelika,* 319 U. S. 103 (1943).

42. *Kunz* v. *New York,* 340 U. S. 290 (1951).

43. *Cantwell* v. *Connecticut,* 310 U. S. 296, at 304, 311 (1940).

44. *Reynolds* v. *United States,* 98 U. S. 145 (1878); *Davis* v. *Beason,* 133 U. S. 333 (1890).

45. *McGowan* v. *Maryland,* 366 U. S. 420 (1961).

46. *Ibid.,* at 575 (dissenting opinion).

47. *Liberty,* January–February, 1962, p. 13.

48. Dr. Sir Muhammed Iqbal, "Presidential Address" delivered at the Allahabad Session of the All-India Muslim League, December 1930, in Gwyer and Appadorai, ed., *Speeches and Documents on the Indian Constitution,* pp. 436-437. Oxford University Press (1957).

49. *Mapp* v. *Ohio,* 367 U. S. 643 (1961).

50. *Olmstead* v. *United States,* 277 U. S. 438 (1928).

51. *Upshaw* v. *United States,* 335 U. S. 410 (1948).

52. See: *Brown* v. *Mississippi,* 297 U. S. 278 (1936); *Chambers* v. *Florida,* 309 U. S. 227 (1940).

53. *Counselman* v. *Hitchcock,* 142 U. S. 547, 562 (1892).

54. *Rogers* v. *United States,* 340 U. S. 367 (1951).

55. *Blau* v. *United States,* 340 U. S. 159 (1950).

56. *Shapiro* v. *United States,* 335 U. S. 1 (1948); *Ullmann* v. *United States,* 350 U. S. 422 (1956).

57. *Quinn* v. *United States,* 349 U. S. 155, 162 (1955).

58. Tennessee Constitution, Art. I, Sec. 9.

59. *The Washington Post and Times-Herald,* April 8, 1962, p. A-10.

60. *In re Oliver,* 333 U. S. 257, 266 (1948).

61. See: *State* v. *Keeler,* 52 Montana 205 (1916).

62. *Reagan* v. *United States,* 202 F. 488 (1913).

63. American Bar Association, *Canons of Judicial Ethics,* No. 35. See also: Federal Rules of Criminal Procedure, Rule No. 53.

64. On the right of confrontation see Trial of Sir Walter Raleigh, 2 How. St. Tr. 1 (1603). On the application of the right of counsel in state criminal trials through the Due Process Clause of the Fourteenth Amendment see *Gideon* v. *Wainwright,* 372 U. S. 335. As respects the right of counsel on appeal in state criminal cases see *Douglas* v. *California,* 372 U. S. 353 (1963).

65. *Virginia* v. *Rives,* 100 U. S. 313, 335 (1879).

66. *Hill* v. *Texas,* 316 U. S. 400 (1942); *Cassell* v. *Texas,* 339 U. S. 282 (1950).

67. *Akins* v. *Texas,* 325 U. S. 398, 403 (1945).

68. *Pierre* v. *Louisiana,* 306 U. S. 354 (1939); *Smith* v. *Texas,* 311 U. S. 128 (1940).

69. *Hill* v. *Texas,* 316 U. S. 400 (1942); *Avery* v. *Georgia,* 345 U. S. 559 (1953). In Georgia, the names of prospective jurors were drawn from a box. Names of white persons appeared on white slips only. Names of Negroes were written on yellow slips. This practice was ended by this decision.

70. *Patton* v. *Mississippi,* 332 U. S. 463, 469 (1947).

71. *Hernandez* v. *Texas,* 347 U. S. 475 (1954).

72. *Report, His Britannic Majesty's Government to the Council of the League of Nations, on the Administration of Iraq* (1926), App. pp. 144 et seq.

73. *Metropolis Theatre Co.* v. *Chicago,* 228 U. S. 61, 69, 70 (1913).

74. *Muller* v. *Oregon,* 208 U. S. 412 (1908); *Miller* v. *Wilson,* 236 U. S. 373 (1915).

75. *West Coast Hotel* v. *Parrish,* 300 U. S. 379 (1937).

76. *Goesaert* v. *Cleary,* 335 U. S. 464, 466 (1948).

77. *Buck* v. *Bell,* 274 U. S. 200 (1927).

78. *Skinner* v. *Oklahoma,* 316 U. S. 535 (1942).

79. *Yick Wo* v. *Hopkins,* 118 U. S. 356, 373 (1886).

80. *Plessy* v. *Ferguson,* 163 U. S. 537 (1896).

81. *Buchanan* v. *Warley,* 245 U. S. 60 (1917).

82. *Shelley* v. *Kraemer,* 334 U. S. 1 (1948).

83. *Barrows* v. *Jackson,* 346 U. S. 249, 254 (1953).

84. *Missouri ex rel. Gaines,* 305 U. S. 337 (1938); and see: *Sipuel* v. *Board of Regents,* 332 U. S. 631 (1948).

85. *Sweatt* v. *Painter,* 339 U. S. 629 (1950).

86. *McLaurin* v. *State Regents,* 339 U. S. 637, at 641, 642 (1950).

87. *Brown* v. *Board of Education,* 347 U. S. 483, 493 (1954); 349 U. S. 294 (1955).

88. *Bolling* v. *Sharpe,* 347 U. S. 497, at 500 (1954).

89. *Mayor of Baltimore City* v. *Dawson,* 350 U. S. 877 (1955); see also: *Dawson* v. *Mayor of Baltimore City,* 220 F2d 386 (1955).

90. *Holmes* v. *City of Atlanta,* 350 U. S. 879 (1955), rev'g. 223 F2d 93 (1955).

91. *Burton* v. *Wilmington Parking Authority,* 365 U. S. 715 (1961).

92. *Thompson* v. *City of Louisville,* 362 U. S. 199 (1960); *Garner* v. *Louisiana,* 368 U. S. 157 (1961).

93. *Gayle* v. *Browder,* 352 U. S. 903 (1956).

94. *State Athletic Commission* v. *Dorsey,* 359 U. S. 533 (1959).

95. *Boynton* v. *Virginia,* 364 U. S. 454 (1960).

96. *Fitzgerald* v. *Pan-American World Airlines,* 229 F2d 499 (1956).

97. *Bailey* v. *Patterson,* 369 U. S. 31 (1962).

98. Executive Order 9981, 13 Fed. Reg. 4313 (1948).

99. Office of the Assistant Secretary of Defense, *Integration in the Armed Services,* p. 9.

100. Joel Barlow, *Advice to the Privileged Orders.* Philadelphia (1792).

101. Duncan, ed., *Selected Writings of Mahatma Gandhi,* p. 169, London (1951).

102. Radhakrishnan, "Inaugural Speech," in *India News,* May 28, 1962, p. 1.

103. Universal Declaration of Human Rights, adopted by General Assembly of the United Nations, December 10, 1948; in *Report on the U. N.,* Department of State Pub. 3437, Int. Org. and Conf. Series III 29, at 204 (1949).

104. Pericles, "On the Causes of Athenian Greatness," in Brewer, ed., *The World's Best Orations,* vol. 8, p. 3170.

CHAPTER II

1. Aristotle, *Politics,* Book IV in R. M. Hutchins, ed., 9 *Great Books of the Western World* 498 et seq. Encyclopaedia Britannica (1952).

2. Massachusetts Bill of Rights, Article XXX (1780), in Commager, *Documents of American History,* p. 107. Appleton-Century-Crofts (1949).

3. Madison, *The Federalist,* No. 51 (February 8, 1788), in Padover, ed., *The Complete Madison,* p. 179. Harper & Bros. (1953).

4. Adams, *The Life and Work of John Adams,* vol. 4, p. 186 (1851).

5. Montesquieu, *The Spirit of the Law,* Book 11, in R. M. Hutchins, ed., 38 *Great Books of the Western World* 70. Encyclopaedia Britannica (1952).

6. U. S. Constitution, Art. I, Sec. 6.

7. Madison, *The Federalist,* No. 48, in Padover, ed., *The Complete Madison,* p. 170. Harper & Bros. (1953).

8. *Wiener* v. *United States,* 357 U. S. 349, 356 (1958).

9. 10 USC 867.

10. *Youngstown Co.* v. *Sawyer,* 343 U. S. 579 (1952).

11. U. S. Constitution, Art. II, Sec. 2.

12. Taft, *Our Chief Magistrate and His Powers,* p. 135. Columbia University Press (1916).

13. *United States* v. *Capps, Inc.,* 348 U. S. 296 (1955).

14. *United States* v. *Pink,* 315 U. S. 203 (1942).

15. See: Borchard, "Shall the Executive Agreement Replace the Treaty?" 54 *Yale L. J.* 664 (1944); Borchard, "Treaties and Executive Agreements: A Reply," 54 *Yale L. J.* 616 (1945).

16. *United States* v. *Curtiss-Wright Export Corp.,* 299 U. S. 304 (1936).

17. See: U. S. Tariff Commission, Operation of the Trade Agreements Program, 1934–1948, Pts. 1-4, Rep. No. 160, Second Series.

18. *Harvard Business Review,* March–April 1962, p. 8.

19. *Clark* v. *Allen,* 331 U. S. 503 (1947).

20. *Oetjen* v. *Central Leather* Co., 246 U. S. 297 (1918).

21. *Jones* v. *United States,* 137 U. S. 202 (1890).

22. *Kennett* v. *Chambers,* 14 How. 38 (1852).

23. *United States* v. *Pink,* 315 U. S. 203 (1942).

24. *Ex parte Peru,* 318 U. S. 578 (1943).

25. *United States* v. *Klein,* 13 Wall. 128, 147 (1871).

26. Samuel Adams, "Letter to the Boston Gazette," December 5, 1768, in Wells, *The Life and Public Services of Samuel Adams,* vol. 1, p. 23. Little, Brown & Co., Boston (1865).

27. See: "A Symposium on Military Justice," 6 *Vand. L. Rev.* 161 et seq. (1961).

28. *Billings* v. *Truesdell,* 321 U. S. 542 (1944).

29. *Coleman* v. *Tennessee,* 97 U. S. 509, 514 (1878).

30. *Whelchel* v. *McDonald,* 340 U. S. 122, 124 (1950).

31. Bennett M. Rich, *The Presidents and Civil Disorder.* Brookings Institution (1941).

32. Washington to Governor Lee, October 20, 1794; in *Federal Aid in Domestic Disturbances,* S. Doc. No. 263, 67th Cong., 2d Sess., p. 31 (1922).

33. U. S. Constitution, Art. I, Sec. 8; U. S. Constitution, Am. 5.

34. *Toth* v. *Quarles,* 350 U. S. 11 (1955).

35. *Reid* v. *Covert,* 354 U. S. 1 (1957); *Kinsella* v. *Singleton* 361 U. S. 234 (1960).

36. *Gresham* v. *Hogan,* 361 U. S. 278 (1960); *McElroy* v. *Guagliardo,* 361 U. S. 281 (1960).

37. *Ex parte Milligan,* 4 Wall. 2 (1866).

38. *Luther* v. *Borden,* 7 How. 1, 45 (1849).

39. U. S. Constitution, Art. I, Sec. 9.

40. L. K. Underhill, "Jurisdiction of Military Tribunals in the U. S. over Civilians," 12 *California L. Rev.* 159, 178.

41. *In re McDonald,* 49 Mont. 454, 476 (1914).

42. *Sterling* v. *Constantin,* 287 U. S. 378 (1932), which in effect overruled *Moyer* v. *Peabody,* 212 U. S. 78.

43. See: Anthony, *Hawaii Under Army Rule,* pp. 64-77, 106. Stanford University Press (1955).

44. *Hirabayashi* v. *United States,* 320 U. S. 81 (1943).

45. *Korematsu* v. *United States,* 323 U. S. 214 (1944).

46. *Ex parte Endo,* 323 U. S. 283 (1944).

47. See: *Ex parte Milligan,* 4 Wall. 1 (1866).

48. Harry S. Truman, "Letter to Harold H. Velde," Chairman House Un-American Activities Committee, in *The New York Times,* November 13, 1953, p. 14.

49. "Impeachment of Andrew Johnson," *Supp. to the Cong. Globe,* 40th Cong., 2d Sess., p. 319 (1868).

50. Taft, *op. cit., supra,* note 12, p. 129.

51. Eisenhower, "Letter to the Secretary of Defense," May 17, 1954, in 100 *Cong. Rec.* 6621 (1954).

52. Bishop, "The Executive's Right of Privacy: An Unresolved Constitutional Question," 66 *Yale L. J.* 477, 491 (1957).

53. Younger, "Congressional Investigations and Executive Secrecy: A Study in the Separation of Powers," 20 *Univ. of Pitts. L. Rev.* 755, 783 (1959).

54. *Report on the Congressional Power of Investigation,* S. Doc. 99, 83d Cong., 2d Sess., p. 27 (1954).

55. See, e.g., *Jencks* v. *United States,* 353 U. S. 657 (1957).

56. *Palermo* v. *United States,* 360 U. S. 343 (1959).

57. *Truman Memoirs,* Vol. II, p. 24. Doubleday (1956).

58. 58 Stat. 190 (1944).

59. Sec. 37 Op. Atty. Gen. 56 (1933).

60. 65 Stat. 336, 365 (1951).

61. H. Rep. No. 1406, 87th Cong., 2d Sess., p. 7 (1962).

62. *The Pocket Veto Case,* 279 U. S. 655 (1929).

63. *United States* v. *Cohen Grocery Co.,* 255 U. S. 81 (1921).

64. *United States* v. *Cardiff,* 344 U. S. 174, 176 (1952).

65. Suetonius, *Lives of the Twelve Caesars,* p. 192. Modern Library (1931).

66. *Schechter Corp.* v. *United States,* 295 U. S. 495 (1935).

67. *Anderson* v. *Dunn,* 6 Wheat. 204, 231 (1821).

68. *Quinn* v. *United States,* 349 U. S. 155, 161 (1955).

69. *McCarthy* v. *Arndstein,* 266 U. S. 34 (1924).

70. *Counselman* v. *Hitchcock,* 142 U. S. 547 (1892).

71. Bagehot, *The English Constitution,* 2d ed., p. 95. Appleton (1952).

72. Jefferson, "Letter to James Madison," March 15, 1789, in Boyd, ed., *The Papers of Thomas Jefferson,* vol. 14, p. 661. Princeton Univ. Press (1958).

73. Madison, *The Federalist,* No. 51, *op. cit., supra,* note 3.

74. De Tocqueville, *Democracy in America,* Bradley, ed., vol. 1, p. 259.

75. *Lochner* v. *New York,* 198 U. S. 45 (1905).

76. *Adkins* v. *Children's Hospital,* 261 U. S. 161 (1923).

77. *Adair* v. *United States,* 208 U. S. 161 (1908).

78. *Day-Brite Lighting, Inc.* v. *Missouri,* 342 U. S. 421, 424-425 (1952).

79. *Berman* v. *Parker,* 348 U. S. 26, 32-33 (1954).

80. *United States* v. *Causby,* 328 U. S. 256 (1946).

81. *Griggs v. Allegheny County,* 369 U. S. 84 (1962).

82. *Green* v. *Frazier,* 253 U. S. 233 (1920).

83. *United States* v. *Miller,* 317 U. S. 369, 373 (1943).

84. *Barry* v. *United States ex rel. Cunningham,* 279 U. S. 597, 616 (1929).

85. Andrews, *Wilson's Works,* vol. 1, pp. 355, 366. Callaghan & Co., Chicago (1896).

86. Rawle, *On the Constitution,* 2d ed., p. 280. Philadelphia (1829).

87. See: *Marbury* v. *Madison,* 1 Cranch 137 (1803).

88. "Impeachment of Samuel Chase," *Annals of Congress,* vol. 14, p. 557, 8th Cong., 2d Sess. (1804–1805).

89. Hearings before the Special Subcommittee to Investigate the Department of Justice. Committee on the Judiciary, House of Representatives, 83d Cong., 1st Sess., *Hearings,* vol. 10898, p. 1753 (May 14–June 30, 1953).

90. U. S. Constitution, Art. III, Sec. 1.

91. *Evans* v. *Gore,* 253 U. S. 245 (1920).

92. *O'Malley* v. *Woodrough,* 307 U. S. 277, 282 (1939).

93. *Marbury* v. *Madison,* 1 Cranch 137, 177 (1803).

94. *United States* v. *Rumely,* 345 U. S. 41 (1953); *United States* v. *Harriss,* 347 U. S. 612 (1954).

95. Madison, "Report on the Virginia Resolutions," in Hunt, ed., *Writings of Madison,* vol. 6, p. 386-387.

96. See: Massachusetts Constitution, Part II, Ch. 3, Art. III; *Opinion of the Justices,* 251 Mass. 569, 147 N. E. 681 (1925).

97. Warren, *The Supreme Court in United States History,* vol. 1, pp. 110, 111. Little, Brown & Co., Boston (1937).

98. *Hayburn's Case,* 2 Dall. 409 (1792).

99. *Massachusetts* v. *Mellon,* 262 U. S. 447 (1923).

100. *Doremus* v. *Board of Education,* 342 U. S. 429 (1952).

101. *Poe* v. *Ullmann,* 367 U. S. 497 (1961).

102. *United Public Workers* v. *Mitchell,* 330 U. S. 75 (1946).

103. *Mitchell* v. *United States,* 313 U. S. 80, 93 (1941).

104. *Evers* v. *Dwyer,* 358 U. S. 202, 204 (1958).

105. *United States* v. *Alaska Steamship Co.,* 253 U. S. 113 (1920).

106. *United States* v. *W. T. Grant Co.,* 345 U. S. 629 (1953).

107. *St. Pierre* v. *United States,* 319 U. S. 41 (1943).

108. *Fiswick* v. *United States,* 329 U. S. 211 (1946).

109. 5 Rotuli Par. 375 at 376.

110. *Nabob* v. *East India Co.,* 1 Ves. Jr. 371 (179–), 2 Ves. Jr. 56 (1792).

111. *Commonwealth* v. *Dennison,* 24 How. 66, 109 (1860).

112. *Clark* v. *Allen,* 331 U. S. 503, 514 (1947).

113. *Oetjen* v. *Central Leather Co.,* 246 U. S. 297 (1918).

114. *Jones* v. *United States,* 137 U. S. 202 (1890).

115. *Clark* v. *Allen,* 331 U. S. 503, 514 (1947).

116. *Ex parte Milligan,* 4 Wall. 2 (1866); *Ex parte Quirin,* 317 U. S. 1 (1942).

117. *C. & S. Air Lines* v. *Waterman Corp.,* 333 U. S. 103 (1948).

118. *Asbury Park Press* v. *Wooley,* 33 N. J. 1, 14 (1960).

119. *Baker* v. *Carr,* 369 U. S. 186 (1962).

120. *Gomillion* v. *Lightfoot,* 364 U. S. 339 (1960).

121. Sir Sarvepalli Radhakrishnan, "Address to Senate," November 17, 1954, in *Cong. Rec.,* v. 100, part 12, p. 16088.

CHAPTER III

1. See: Brown and Real, *Community of Fear.* The Center for the Study of Democratic Institutions, Santa Barbara, Calif. (1960).

2. Bethe, with McDonald, in *Science,* One of a Series of Interviews on the American Character. The Center for the Study of Democratic Institutions, Santa Barbara, Calif. (1962).

3. Eatherly, quoted by Wechsler, in "The Hero of Hiroshima," *The Progressive,* p. 47 (Feb. 1962).

4. Pauling, in *The Washington Post,* Feb. 26, 1962, p. A-10, col. 5-6.

Not all of these mutations will be obvious: "Mutations which have a mild effect on the individual may cause substantial damage in the aggregate. This is because the mildness permits these mutations, such as slight reductions in viability and other less obvious effects, to persist in the population longer than mutations with severe effects, and thus to affect a correspondingly greater number of persons. There are no data which would permit these effects to be assessed with sufficient accuracy to permit numerical estimates." Report of the Federal Radiation Council, *The New York Times,* June 2, 1962, p. 6, col. 4.

5. United Nations Charter, Preamble.

6. Millis, *A World Without War.* The Center for the Study of Democratic Institutions, Santa Barbara, Calif. (1961).

7. Blackett, "Steps Towards Disarmament," in *The Scientific American,* vol. 206, p. 45 (April 1962).

8. Wilson, *One Chinese Moon,* Hill and Wang, New York (1961).

9. See: Moraes, *The Revolt in Tibet,* Macmillan, New York (1960).

10. Moore, *International Law,* vol. 1, p. 107. Washington (1906).

11. Hyde, *International Law,* 2d ed., vol. 1, p. 161. Little, Brown & Co., Boston (1945).

12. Jessup, *A Modern Law of Nations,* p. 57. Macmillan, New York (1948).

13. Oppenheim, *International Law,* Lauterpacht, ed., 8th ed., p. 133. Longmans Green & Co., London (1955).

14. See: Hobbes, *Leviathan,* Part I, Ch. XV (1651).

15. Austin, "Province of Jurisprudence Determined," in Robert Campbell, ed., *Lectures on Jurisprudence,* 5th ed. London (1885).

16. See: Clark and Sohn, *World Peace Through World Law.* Harvard University Press, Cambridge (1960).

17. Grotius, *De jure belli ac pacis,* Prolegomena, Sec. 1.

18. Marcus Aurelius, *Meditations,* Book IV; in 12 *Great Books* 264. Encyclopaedia Britannica (1952).

19. Cohen, *The United Nations,* p. 88. Harvard University Press, Cambridge (1961).

20. *Ibid.*

21. *United Nations Yearbook 1950,* p. 224. Columbia University Press, in co-operation with the United Nations.

22. Cohen, *op. cit., supra,* note 19, p. 18.

23. Jawaharlal Nehru, quoted in *The Reporter,* Jan. 4, 1962, vol. 26, no. 1, p. 10.

24. *Certain Expenses of the United Nations,* Advisory Opinion of July 20, 1962, I. C. J. Reports 1962.

If the Court's advisory opinion is accepted by the General Assembly, the defaulting countries will have to pay at least part of the assessments for the Middle East and Congo operations within the next two years. Article 19 of the Charter provides that if the amount owed by a member state "equals or exceeds the amount of the contributions due from it" for the past two years, that state shall lose its vote in the General Assembly. This sanction has to date proved effective.

25. *Kolovrat* v. *Oregon,* 366 U. S. 187 (1960).

26. *United States* v. *Pink,* 315 U. S. 203 (1942).

27. *Ex parte Quirin,* 317 U. S. 1 (1942).

28. *The Paquette Hobana,* 175 U. S. 677 (1900).

29. *Schooner Exchange* v. *M'Fadden,* 7 Cranch 116 (1812).

30. *Hines* v. *Davidowitz,* 312 U. S. 52 (1941)

31. *United States* v. *California,* 332 U. S. 19 (1947).

32. *Fisheries case,* Judgment of Dec. 18, 1951, I. C. J. Rep. 1951, p. 116.

33. *United States* v. *Louisiana,* 363 U. S. 1 (1959).

34. Sohn, "International Tribunals, Past, Present, and Future," 46 *A.B.A. Journ.* 23 (Jan. 1960).

35. See: Jay Treaty, Art. V; Moore, *International Arbitration,* vol. 1, pp. 5-6 (1898).

36. McNair, *The Development of International Justice,* p. 2. New York Univ. Press (1954).

37. *Ryan* v. *United States,* 32 *Am. J. Int'l. Law* 593, 595.

38. *Treaty with China,* Nov. 4, 1946, Art. VI, Sec. 4; in 63 Stat. 1299, 1300, Part 2, 81st Cong., 1st Sess. (1949).

39. Individuals in mandated territories have, however, the right to petition the mandatory governments; and the latter have an obligation to forward the petitions to the appropriate agencies of the United Nations. See: *International Status of Southwest Africa,* I. C. J. Rep. 1950, p. 128; *Admissibility of Hearings of Petitioners,* I. C. J. Rep. 1956, p. 23.

40. *Anglo-Iranian Oil Co. case* (jurisdiction), Judgment of July 22, 1952: I. C. J. Rep. 1952, pp. 93, 112.

41. Statute of the International Court of Justice, Art. 9.

42. United Nations Charter, Art. 94, Sec. 2.

43. United Nations Charter, Art. 96. For advisory opinions of the Court see: *Reparation for Injuries Suffered in the Service of the U. N.,* I. C. J. Rep. 1949, p. 174; *Admissibility of Hearings of Petitioners, supra,* note 39; *Judgments of the Administrative Tribunal of ILO,* J. C. J. Rep. 1956, p. 77.

44. See: *Guide to the United Nations Charter,* pp. 46-47. U. N. Publications Sales No. 1947.1.16 (1947).

45. *Declaration by the President,* August 14, 1946; in 61 Stat. 1218, Part 2, 80th Cong., 1st Sess. (1947).

46. Sen. Wayne Morse, in 92 *Cong. Rec.* 10684, Part 8, 79th Cong., 2d Sess., Jul.–Aug. 1946.

47. *Case of Certain Norwegian Loans:* Judgment of July 6, 1957, I. C. J. Rep. 1957, p. 9.

48. Sohn, "International Tribunals: Past, Present, and Future," 46 *A. B. A. Journ.* 23, 25 (Jan. 1960).

49. Jessup, *The Use of International Law,* p. 60. Univ. Mich. Press (1959).

50. Eisenhower, "The Role of Lawyers in Promoting the Rule of Law," 46 *A. B. A. Journ.* 1095 (Oct. 1960).

51. See: *Interhandel case,* Judgment of March 21st, 1959: I. C. J. Rep. 1959, p. 6; Briggs, "Interhandel: The Courts' Judgment on the Preliminary Objections of the U. S.," 53 *Am. J. Int'l. Law* 547.

52. *Interhandel case,* dissenting opinion, I. C. J. Rep. 1959, pp. 54, 59.

53. But even these countries have adopted new reservations which are restrictive of the Court's jurisdiction. England, for example, reserved nine specific subjects, among those being "disputes arising out of, or having reference to, any hostilities, war, state of war, or belligerent or military occupation in which the Government of the United Kingdom are or have been involved." England also reserved the right "at any time . . . to add to, amend, or withdraw" any of its reservations, to take effect from the moment of notification. I. C. J. Yearbook 1959–1960, pp. 254, 255.

After July 1, 1963, France was able to withdraw from the Court's jurisdiction whenever she chose. Of the thirty-nine adherents to its jurisdiction, twenty-three have reserved the right to withdraw at will, in contrast to the United States' provision for a six months' notice of withdrawal. *Ibid.,* 233-255. See Baldwin, "An Alternative to the Connally Amendment as a Practical and Realistic Step Toward World Peace Through Law," 13 *S. C. L. Q.* 516 (1961).

54. See: *Nebraska* v. *Wyoming,* 325 U. S. 589 (1945).

55. See: Caroe, "The Geography and Ethnics of India's Northern Frontiers," 126 *Geogr. J.* 298 (Sept. 1960); Caroe, "The Indian-Chinese Border Dispute," 127 *Geogr. J.* 345 (Sept. 1961).

56. The Indian position against China invoked the watershed principle: "Various international authorities of different countries, commenting on traditional boundaries, have testified to the logic of the watershed principle; and it is now a well-recognized principle of customary international law that when two countries are separated by a mountain range and there are no boundary treaties or specified agreements, the traditional boundary tends to take

shape along the crest which divides the major volume of the waters flowing into the two countries. The innate logic of this principle is self-evident. The inhabitants of the two areas not only tend to settle up to the intervening barrier but wish and seek to retain control of the drainage basins." *Report of the Indian Officials on the Boundary Question,* concluding chapter (MEA 30), p. 4 (1961).

57. See: *Nebraska* v. *Iowa,* 143 U. S. 359 (1892).

58. *Fisheries case,* Judgment of Dec. 1951: I. C. J. Rep. 1951, p. 116.

59. Statute of the International Court of Justice, Art. 38, Sec. a-d; Art. 59.

60. See: De Carn, "The Connally Amendment," in *National Review,* March 11, 1961, pp. 143 et seq.

61. Lauterpacht, *International Law and Human Rights,* p. 70. Praeger, New York (1950).

62. *Ibid.,* pp. 409, 410. Lauchterpacht's view of human rights was given fresh significance when the International Court ruled recently by an 8–7 vote that it had jurisdiction to hear a case dealing with racial discrimination in South West Africa. The latter is a former German colony, now administered by South Africa, and the case was brought before the Court by Ethiopia and Liberia, who seek to end the segregated policies in this territory. *South West Africa Cases (Ethiopia* v. *South Africa; Liberia* v. *South Africa), Preliminary Objections,* Judgment of 21 December 1962: I. C. J. Reports 1962, p. 319.

63. Statute of the International Court of Justice, Art. 34, Sec. 1.

64. Cohen, *op cit., supra,* note 19, p. 59.

65. Hammarskjöld, 8 *U. N. Review* 12, 16.

66. "Declaration of the Rights of the Child," Preamble, *Yearbook of the United Nations 1959,* p. 198.

67. "This organization has at present no function whatsoever, and if it is maintained in existence at all, it should be maintained as an exercise in cooperation among nations.

"The first director of this agency was an American, and his term expired recently. Since, next to America, the Soviet Union is the most important atomic power, America could have proposed that the next director of the agency be a Russian. Instead, America proposed a Swede, who was not acceptable to the Russians, and since America had the votes she was able to win one more victory in a meaningless battle of the cold war." Szilard, "Are We on the Road to War?" *Bulletin of the Atomic Scientists,* v. 18, pp. 23, 26 (April 1962).

68. Senator Henry M. Jackson, "Speech to the National Press

Club," quoted in *The New York Times,* March 21, 1962, p. 1, col. 7.

    69. Mao Tse-tung, *Selected Works,* p. 176. Lawrence & Wishart, Ltd., London (1954).

CHAPTER IV

    1. See: "COMECON vs. Common Market," *The Christian Science Monitor,* June 2, 1962, p. 18, col. 1; *The Washington, D. C., Sunday Star,* June 10, 1962, p. E-10, col. 1.

    2. Charter of the Organization of American States, Art. 21.

    3. *Ibid.,* Art. 16.

    4. *Ibid.,* Art. 4.

    5. *Ibid.,* Art. 112.

    6. *Ibid.,* Art. 111, Art. 109.

    7. Statement of Mexico, Organization of American States, 8th Meeting of Consultation of Ministers, Jan. 31, 1962, Doc. 68, p. 24.

    8. Address by Francisco Clemention de Santiago Dantas, Brazilian Minister of Foreign Affairs, Organization of American States, 8th Meeting of Consultation of Ministers, Jan. 24, 1962, Doc. 32.

    9. There is danger that once Castro is made a force against which the might and power of this hemisphere is arrayed, he will emerge as a lengendary Robin Hood. South America is plagued with poverty. The extremes of wealth are as great there as in Iran, Saudi Arabia, and Ethiopia. The conditions which nurture that poverty gave rise to Castro. Unless political action creates hope that they will soon be removed, more Castros are likely. The important provision of the OAS Charter is Article 29, which commits the member states to the goal of giving all human beings "the right to attain material well-being and spiritual growth under circumstances of liberty, dignity, equality of opportunity, and economic security"; and of providing the conditions for work "that ensure life, health, and a decent standard of living, both during the working years and during old age, or when any circumstances deprive the individual of the possibility of working."

    10. See: "The European Convention for the Protection of Human Rights and Fundamental Freedoms," in 49 *Calif. L. Rev.* 172 (1961).

    11. "The European Commission of Human Rights," 50 *Am. J. Int'l. Law* 949 (1956); Waldock, "European Convention for Human Rights," *British Yearbook of Int'l Law 1958,* p. 356.

12. The European Convention for the Protection of Human Rights, and Fundamental Freedoms.

13. See: *European Commission of Human Rights, Documents and Decisions,* pp. vi, 132 (1959).

14. *Ibid.,* pp. 219-226.

15. "Convention Relating to Certain Institutions Common to the European Communities," 51 *Am. J. Int'l. Law,* pp. 1001-1003 (1957); Part II, "The Court of Justice," pp. 1001-1003.

16. See: Christol, "Remedies for Individuals Under World Law," 56 *Northwestern Univ. L. Rev.* 65, 72-80 (1961).

17. See: Stein, "The Court of Justice, 1954–1957," 51 *Am. J. Int'l. Law,* pp. 821, 829; "Groupement des Ind. Sid. Lux *v.* The High Authority," *Official Gazette,* July 10, 1956, 5th Year, No. 16, p. 190.

18. For an account of ideological and administrative matters that have made COMECON awkward and inefficient, see Toma, "The Communists and the Common Market," Progressive.

19. This idea of the rich getting richer and the poor, poorer is not a fantasy. A 1962 Report shows that three decades after the Big Depression the wealthiest one per cent of American adults own 28 per cent of the nation's total personal wealth, which is only slightly less than that held in 1933. The poorest one-third now own only one per cent. Ninety per cent of the population, which includes the affluent middle class, owns less than half of that wealth. In 1929, ownership of 65.6 per cent of corporate stock was held by the top one per cent; by 1953, that had increased to 76 per cent; and the trend was still upward. As compared with 27,000 millionaires in the United States in 1953, there were over 100,000 in 1962. In 1953, there were 2,113 individuals whose wealth exceeded five million each. In 1962, there are over 100,000. Lampman, *The Share of Top Wealth-Holders in National Wealth.* Princeton Univ. Press (1962).

For conditions in Mexico, see *Income Distribution and Economic Development of Mexico* by Ifigenia Navarrete. Mrs. Navarrete reports that between 1950 and 1957 Mexico's industrialization greatly benefited the growing middle class, but it also let the rich get richer and the poor get poorer. While over-all family incomes rose 23 per cent, the bottom one-fifth of Mexican families' share of national income dropped from 6.1 per cent to 4.4 per cent, and their average monthly earnings fell from $22.00 to $19.80. The next 30 per cent of Mexican families, just a cut above them, barely managed to maintain their 1950 income levels.

The biggest rewards of industrialization, which sent gross national product soaring 48 per cent in the seven years, went to the top 30 per cent of Mexican families, who increased their real income by some 30 per cent. The topmost 5 per cent did best of all, skimming off 37 per cent of national income in 1957.

The losers by industrialization were mostly unskilled farm laborers driven from the land by mechanization and drawn to the cities.

20. Kravis, "The Common Market—Lesson in Trade Expansion," *Harvard Bus. Rev.*, p. 7 (March–April 1962).

21. *9 Psychiatry 3*, 20.

22. *Graham* v. *United States*, 231 U. S. 474, 480 (1913).

23. Strausz-Hupe and Kintner, "Military Defense: Free World Strategy in the '60's," *The General Electric Forum*, vol. 5, no. 1, p. 23 (Jan.–March 1962).

24. *Communism, The Nature of Your Enemy*, John Jessup, ed., and the editors of *Life*, p. 73. Time, Inc. (1962).

25. Halle, *Men and Nations*, p. 108. Princeton Univ. Press (1962).

26. *Ibid.*, p. 109.

27. Carl Becker, *The Declaration of Independence*, p. 278. Knopf (1962).

28. Freud, Sigmund, *Civilization and Its Discontents* (1929).